SPIRITUAL
FITNESS

ARE YOU READY
FOR THE BEST
SELF-MASTERY CHALLENGE
OF YOUR LIFE?

Jean-Pierre De Villiers

WM

Spiritual Fitness

Jean-Pierre De Villiers

First published in September 2020

WM Publishing

ISBN 978-1-912774-67-8

Contents

Why Make Your Spiritual Fitness A Priority?

Andrew Priestley

People *say* their health is the most important thing but the reality is good health probably isn't until you get a nudge or find your health compromised.

Last year, I was 13+ stone and when I went for a check up my metabolic age was ten years older than my chronological age. That was a shock but the wake-up call came after seeing photos of myself speaking at a book launch looking old and tired.

So, I decided to make my health a priority.

I started running – shuffling really. Then doing pushups. I also bought a DVD fitness programme and committed to a daily 25-minute high intensity workout. In addition, I rebooted my meditation and mindfulness practices, sorted out my diet, increased my fresh water intake; and started small habits like no devices after 8pm or before 9am.

I am not sure why but I've actually stuck with it.

See, I thought health was a choice, on my to-do list once I sorted other priorities.

Then I got word that my good friend JP had been critically injured in a drunk driver hit-and-run accident while cycling to raise money for a charity, for God's sake! He was fighting for his life. This is someone who has health as his highest priority and walks his talk. Someone who's in supreme physical and mental condition suddenly in intensive care, having operations and having his limbs reinforced with steel rods. Health became his *only* choice.

It was enough for me to not only place my own health at the top of my list, but to follow through.

Incredibly, JP's commitment to health has him on the road to recovery faster and sooner than anyone can dare imagine and while his athletic career is still being determined, he has recovered full use of his limbs and looks like a fighter again.

His commitment to health hadn't changed and his physical stretch goal this time is climbing Mt. Kilimanjaro.

What has changed is a deepening of his commitment to spiritual fitness. The message of this book is simple – pick a big physical stretch goal and then use the strategies described to support mind, body and heart through a process designed to cultivate a spiritual fitness and to take you onwards to a richer and more fulfilling life.

I hope you read this book many times. Engage with its message. Make your health a conscious, deliberate priority. I know this book will inspire you to start taking practical steps now towards a healthier mind, body and heart; and to make spiritual fitness part of your lifelong journey.

Andrew Priestley

Business Leadership Coach / Author / Speaker

'Yeah Baby!'

First of all thank you for buying my book. This book is about *changing your energy, changing your life.*

I want you to fully engage with this book so right now grab a pen and let me know that you are clearly ready to *change your energy and change your life.* At the top of this page write a two-word response. *Yeah, baby!* And then we'll get started.

Do it right now.

I'm going to be sharing two big stories with you, teaching you, and I'm also going to share one very, very powerful tool that I promise you, if you never hear from me, or see me again, this tool will potentially change your life. Not just once. Again and again and again and again.

And I didn't read this in a textbook. I'm not a textbook coach or speaker. I don't have a real qualification to my name but I have a shedload of life experience, and some very practical strategies and hacks. And you're soon about to read about some of my life's experiences.

So, let's get into it. And if you're already excited write, *Let's go!*

Part 1

Stretch!

v. to cause something to reach, often as far as possible, in a particular direction

v. (of something soft or elastic)
be made or be capable of being made longer or wider without tearing or breaking.

Cape Town To Party Town

I live in the UK but I'm not from the UK. I'm from Cape Town, South Africa.

I didn't have the worst life growing up, but it wasn't a life I would wish upon anyone else.

I went to eight different schools and we moved around a lot. As a result of not having a lot of certainty in my life, I grew up with the opposite... uncertainty, and slowly as I became conditioned in the first few years of my life... I started to hide away from life, more and more and more.

And then at the age of 13, I found a strategy for me to get more certainty. Without even knowing it, I'd found my first personal development tool, or even my first self-mastery tool.

It was fitness. Fitness changed my life.

I tried so many sports... and then I found cycling!

It didn't matter what was going on at home, or what was going on at school, I knew if I climbed on my bike, everything was good. Everything was good when I was out in fitness.

Now, we didn't have a lot of money so I didn't have a very good bike but I always did the best with what I had.

When I used to surf (before I found cycling) I had big holes in my wetsuit and as I went under a wave I would just hold onto my wetsuit because the cold water just went straight through my wetsuit!

Sports really changed my life.

I'm so glad I grew up in South Africa because sport is a big part of our culture. Actually my greatest hero, someone that we all know... the late, great Nelson Mandela said, *Sport has the power to change the world.*

If you want to change *the* world, it starts with changing *your* world.

So I immersed myself in sports. I immersed myself in this strategy. But what I was doing without knowing it then was that I was running *away from* something more than running *towards* something.

At 19 years of age when I left school, I stopped being bullied, I moved to a new area and I got my first full-time job. I actually started working part-time at the age of 10. I almost went to foster care at 10 because my mother couldn't afford to take care of us at the time but at 10 years old I started washing car windows at a petrol station with my brother. At 11 years of age I was delivering newspapers, washing cars and selling sweets door-to-door. And at 12 I started pushing shopping trolleys for tips. But at 19 years old I got my first proper job. And I started going out in Cape Town.

I'll never ever forget when I found my second strategy for feeling good. I went out to a nightclub and the name of the club was *Adrenaline.*

Now you can only imagine, with a name like *Adrenaline,* what kind of things went on in that club. It was unhealthy for sure, but I found my next strategy. I found my next way for me to feel good.

Like the cycling it became my survival mechanism. It was my survival tool.

I went all-in partying; and then became a DJ. After getting into clubbing at 19 in Cape Town, knowing I was never going to be a pro-cyclist, I realised that I wanted to be a DJ, because I loved the music… it made me feel good. And the lifestyle did too, or so I thought.

I wanted to be a superstar DJ, so I moved to the UK. I first got a job in a chicken factory, then a dog food factory and a job job as a waiter. Slowly, slowly I moved my way up to being a DJ. By the age of 23 years old I was a professional DJ - full time - being paid a lot of money.

At the end of that year I reached the pinnacle in my DJ career. I was DJing in Riga, Latvia. I was staying at the Radisson Hotel. Now, keep in mind that at 20 I went to the UK on my own, leaving South Africa for the first time ever, on an aeroplane for the first time ever… and now three years later I'm in a Radisson Hotel, with a driver to pick me up at the airport, being told to come to the club one hour before midnight. I get to the club, I play to 2,500 people. I'm a god! I'm a rock star! But the next morning I felt exactly the opposite. I went from a rock star to rock bottom.

And I thought, *Is this it? Is this my life?*

You see, I couldn't blame anyone because I got on that plane to the UK on my own. I was out of school. I was an adult. It was no one's fault for getting my life wrong. It was totally mine.

13

But I was very aware in that moment that I was getting life wrong. I was toxic. Drunk, high and alone.

And it reminded me of exactly ten years before that moment. The 27th of July is my birthday. Also shared by my father. I was *his* birthday present.

Just after my 13th birthday (I started cycling at 13), I did a cycling race and I won that race. I won.

When I came home and I couldn't wait to tell my mother and my stepfather. And eventually my father. He was my hero. I was a child, so of course he was my hero... but he wasn't a perfect man. I was looking forward to getting home and telling my mom and my stepfather. Then I couldn't wait to eventually get on the phone tell my dad.

When I got around the final corner to my stepfather's house... the South African police (SAP) were at the front door speaking to my Mom. My mom said, *Go inside.*

I went straight inside to my mother's room. There was Andre, my younger brother, and Sean, my youngest brother. And on the bed we sat there white faced like ghosts waiting to be told what was going on and eventually my mother came in, sat down and said, *I'm so sorry, your Dad's dead.*

My father had gone to a beach that I used to surf at called Big Bay. He had driven into the sand dunes and taken his own life.

Now, back to me being 23 years old.

I'm doing life on my own. I'm responsible for my own actions because I'm an adult. Well let's say a grown up, because we all know adults that aren't grown ups right? And I realised that I have a choice in this moment.

14

Continue to get life wrong … or figure out how to get it right. And the reason why I knew I could get it right was because I came to the UK, to London - neutral - with about £20. I had a job waiting for me and even though it was working on a conveyor belt in a chicken factory, it was a job.

I came with nothing. I came neutral. And I got myself to where I was.

So, I thought, if I could get myself where I am now, I've just got to figure out how I can go in a *new* direction.

After picking myself up, wiping myself off and scraping off the toxicity, off and out of my body… I went back to the UK and found a Coach.

Three Tools
That Changed My Life

My story - my success - didn't happen in rapid succession. It took time, even though it might seem like it just happened overnight. There are no overnight successes.

I'm in my late thirties now and I'm still learning… I'm still growing.

I got a coach when I was 23 and he said, *JP, do these three things.*

He told me to do these three things which were the first steps in me changing my life. Write them down. Highlight them.

Number one, *JP, you need a mentor. You need someone to look up to, to aspire to be like, to guide you, to challenge you and to tell you the truth.*

He said, *I want you to write down this name.*

I wrote down the name, *Tony Robbins.* Actually, back then it was Anthony Robbins. I started to study Tony Robbins from that day onwards.

Second thing he said was, *JP, you need to change your*

environment. You need to start changing where you are spending your energy... and start investing your energy.

This book is all about energy.

I started to change my environment by looking specifically at what gave me energy. *What gave me energy? What was a drain on my energy? What was stealing energy from me?*

Before we go any further, I want you to get your mobile phone, locate your voice recorder and for the next seven minutes, just start talking about the things that *give* you energy. *What lights you up? What gives you a boost?*

(And let's be clear: segment that list into good and bad stuff! Alcohol or drugs might give you energy... but it's not good for you.)

Then make a list of what *steals* your energy. Substances, behaviours, habits, people, situations...

Looking back at my life, sport and fitness always gave me energy. So I started going back to the gym and getting back into fitness.

The third thing he said was, *JP, you've got to mind your thoughts.* He said, *I want you to come to my house and watch this DVD. It's very cheesy, but listen to the words.*

Can you guess what that DVD was? It was about the power of thoughts. It was about the law of attraction, and that everything we think - *everything* - not some things, but everything we think... we become.

It was called *The Secret.*

And both the DVD and then that book *helped* me. It didn't change my life. Tony didn't change my life. Changing my environment and who I surrounded myself with didn't change my life. But they *helped* me do it.

They were my new tools. My new strategies for change and a better life.

These tools were so empowering. Crazy empowering. Because never before in my life before did I have a conversation about positive mindset, goals, reaching your full potential, following your intuition or listening to your inner voice. No one ever told me about that stuff.

No one ever said to me think positive. That's no exaggeration. Not one person.

Maybe this is you. Maybe no one has been there for you in that way, but it's never too late. I say that not because I changed my life at 23, I say that because I *continue* to change my life, my energy, every single year.

And with just those three tools - my mentor, changing my environment (aligning it to be supportive of who I wanted to become) – I started to mind my thinking. I *radically* changed my life.

After two and a half years, I was on top of the world, sharing with my friends. *Just do this. Think different. Get into fitness. Workout every day. Have positive and empowering habits. Get a mentor like Tony Robbins.*

After two and a half years I realised, *Man, I have so many tools here. I can help someone else do this. I can help someone else change their life.*

Maybe, just maybe (there are no guarantees in life) if my father knew what I knew, maybe he'd still be here.

I stood in that moment of realisation, in the gym, and I knew that for the rest of my life - because of the tools and awareness I had, I had a true calling and a higher purpose. I had to keep learning and keep sharing what I knew.

I had an obligation to share those tools.

I'm here as a student of life and self-mastery and an informed human being that cares deeply about people's existence. Yours.

I do my very best wherever I go to take people from suffering… to surviving… to thriving.

And it starts with your energy.

Crash!

At 25, I made a career out of it and I've been doing it ever since.

I'm in my late 30s and I've taught self-mastery in 16 countries. I've written multiple books and been on the cover of magazines. I've done all right. I've lived a good life. I've traveled business class, even first class. I don't really care about any of that stuff. I'm just mentioning it because sometimes people want to hear it for credibility reasons. If you want to see more about me, what I do and what I stand for then you can find me on social media. I document all of my life, the good, the bad and the ugly. And let me tell you, last year, my life got ugly.

Very ugly.

One of the things I've done well in my life, at least in my adult life from the age of 23 when I decided that I was going to *continuously* work on bettering myself... and *becoming* a better version of myself... a better leader in *every single area of my life*... was I started to face my fears. Fears are not real. I'm sure you know that saying: FEAR is *False Evidence Appearing Real.*

And if you change the association to fear, you can *Face Everything And Rise.*

Every time I identified a fear I would attack it. Fear? Attack! Fear? Attack! I was scared of confrontation because of 12 years of bullying. So what did I do? I became a boxer and Thai boxer. I was scared of fighting and I took that to the highest level I could, I became a professional Muay Thai fighter. I fought in stadiums in the UK and I've fought in a stadium in Thailand.

I was scared of being the centre of attention because of how it was treated as a kid, and even had my best friends turning on me in school. So what did I do? I became a speaker.

I used to be massively scared of heights. Today, I've done cliff jumps, bungee jumps and I've skydived twice.

I took my sports and fitness to the highest level I could. I became an Ironman triathlete. I've done the hardest Ironman in the world - Ironman Wales. I ran the Cape Peninsula in under 2 days, 145km, and I finished on top of Table Mountain. And I just took a moment there for myself.

All of these experiences that made me uncomfortable were about one thing.

And that's becoming. *Becoming.* Life is about exactly that. Becoming.

So let me ask you this question. Just think about it for now. *Who do you want to become? And what do you need to do to become that person, whoever it is that you want to be?*

I've become a lot over the years and I'm living more today in my highest truth than I ever have. I know who I am and what I stand for.

Something that became a big part of my life and is one of

my highest values (I started to live more and more in my own values over the years) is *contribution*. That's what gives me energy. *Giving* gives me energy. And by the way, a secret, it's the same for all of us.

Giving gives us energy.

What you do for others is what you do for yourself. And that's why I love *Ubuntu*, which means *I am because of you, you are because of me, and we are because of each other.*

So, with contribution as one of my highest values, I started to do a lot of charity work. I've raised hundreds of thousands for charity. And in 2019, I decided to take a coaching client through a physical, mental, emotional and spiritual stretch goal - to cycle the length of the UK, 1000 miles (just over 1,600 kilometres) from the north, through Scotland, England and Wales and finish at Lands End, the southern tip of the UK. And at the end of Day 7, we had our team huddle while having a vegan pizza, and my assistant Signe Ilse says, *JP, we're in a little bit of trouble. Because you've marketed this whole charity event as 1000 miles in 10 days, I don't know what you guys have done but we're running out of miles.*

Do you believe that there are no such things as accidents in life? That everything happens for a reason? Write *Yes* in your book if you believe that.

There are no accidents. Everything happens for a reason.

To come back to the story, I'm saying, *Oh, what are we going to do? We told everyone it's 1,000 miles. We can't finish less than 1,000 miles.* So I say, *Let's go around that way* (pointing my finger at the map).

And that's how much thought we put into it. At the touch of a finger, I changed the whole trajectory of my life.

The next day we went on a new route that wasn't planned or foreseen. And what happened was…

There were loads of hills. Every day prior to that day, having cycled over 100 miles a day, we were usually finished by seven o'clock. But because of all the hills at this new uninvestigated route, we ended up still cycling at 7pm.

And then… 10 minutes past 7pm on the eighth day of the cycle challenge, whilst going down a hill about 40 mile an hour (70km an hour) a car came up the hill at the same speed and hit me head on.

I went flying over the road. I broke all sorts of bones in my body. My bike smashed into pieces. If you know my story, you've seen the pictures. And if you want to know the story of the accident, all you have to do, because it got massive press coverage because of my career, is type in *JP De Villiers Accident*, and you'll find it all there.

I'm broken. My bike is broken. I'm lucky that I didn't fall further down the hill because I got stopped by a tree and I was left between a road barrier and the tree.

The driver just kept on driving. It was a hit and run. And I was literally left for dead on the side of the road.

There are no accidents. You have to believe that. To change the experience of everything that's going on.

And I'm saying, nothing happens by accident.

At that accident site the first person to stop was a paramedic. The next person to stop was an off-duty police officer. And the third person to stop was from National Sea Rescue who just happened to have a tank of oxygen in his car.

Well, how lucky could I be? A miracle indeed and rare. A miracle indeed.

A helicopter came to get me. I was flown to trauma hospital. I spent two weeks in intensive care. I broke both my legs in multiple places. I've got titanium rods from my hip down to my knee and from my knee down to my ankle. I smashed my arm. It was wrapped around me. My leg was wrapped behind me. I punctured and collapsed my lung. I've got a scar up my stomach. Actually, I've got scars everywhere.

Then in intensive care I got even worse. My heart was erratic. I developed a chest infection. And at one point I even stopped breathing.

Eventually, after 10 or 11 days, I started to become fully conscious. I was in and out of consciousness before that because I was on a lot of morphine and experienced a lot of trauma that I was having to deal with. When I could start to understand what was going on, the doctors and the consultants started to talk to me and say things like…

Do you believe in God?

Don't worry, I'm not going all religious on you. This is just what they said. *Someone was watching over you that day.*

And the doctor that worked on me said, *You're obviously very strong in your mind… and you must be very fit because you've been fighting to keep your life.*

When I started to become fully conscious, I just started to think so many things and one of the things I thought was, *Thank God.*

I had all the tools.

Thank God I'd been putting tools in my toolbox since I was 23 years old, because I knew how I was going to deal with this. Head on! Since then, I've been told when I've had tests - *You're a perfect specimen* (being playful of course!)

Two months after leaving hospital my orthopaedic surgeon said, *JP I don't know what to tell you. Your bones are healed. We have no reason to see you anymore.*

I've also been told, *You're a medical wonder, how did you recover so quickly?*

And my lawyer said to me, *JP you don't understand. You think we are flattering you. The way you are after seven months it usually takes our other clients, two or three years to get there.*

Why am I sharing this with you?

Not to tell you that I'm superhuman. I'm not. I'm exactly like you. You know a bit of my story. I've barely given you a grain of sand of my whole story. But what I am telling you is that I'm no different to you. I have just invested my life in *energy management*, personal leadership and self-mastery. And I was able to take all of those tools I'd accumulated in my life and the moment I became fully conscious and opened my eyes after my accident, the moment I was fully aware, I started going to work on myself.

You Create The Meaning

I started to say things like, This didn't happen *to* me. This happened *for* me.

It wasn't the driver's fault for driving into me and leaving me for dead. It was my fault for choosing that route. I never blamed anyone else for what happened.

By making myself responsible, it gave me the power to choose any meaning of that experience. Most people already know that life has absolutely no meaning until we give it meaning. Life itself has no meaning until we come into it. For example, if three people with the same life had to write down the meaning of life, the words would all be different. So, what does that tell us? We create our meaning. We create our life. I started to create the meaning of this life experience.

I started to work on the three aspects of my energy. We have three energy parts: our **mind**, our **body**, and our **heart.**

I knew that *everything is energy* and *energy is everything* and *where energy goes energy flows.*

I knew that right now, more than ever, I had to be super clear, aware and conscious of what energy I was giving myself.

As I lay in my hospital bed, I went to work in these three areas of mind, body and heart.

I started to ask myself… What do I want to do to feel positive energy as opposed to a negative energy through my *attention* and *intention*. What do I want to do in my recovery to add to myself, rather than *take away.*

I asked myself the right questions every day.

I created the meaning.

Spiritual Fitness

People said my recovery seemed miraculous, but it wasn't luck. It wasn't an accident, it wasn't by chance. It was by design. I designed my life to be able to thrive through that massive time of uncertainty.

Why did my recovery and attitude during this time seem so extraordinary? Not just because of my physical fitness.

It was my *spiritual fitness.*

What saved my life was my physical fitness. But what continued to help me heal, transform and reinvent myself and show up with optimism, enthusiasm and gratitude, even in my darkest and most difficult moments, was my spiritual fitness.

Let's bring you back to fitness.

The definition of fitness is a *state of readiness.* When you look at physical fitness, your fitness in the *physical* area is your *state of physical readiness.*

So, what is spiritual fitness? It's your *state of spiritual readiness.* It's your ability to be present, your ability to stay in the present moment, in the now, without being unsettled too much that you're living in the future, chasing something, or living in the past, running away from something.

Spiritual fitness has been one of the greatest tools in my life.

Let me ask you these questions:

How spiritually fit are you?

How fit is your spirit?

Stretch Goals

Think about a situation that you're in right now, whatever it may be.

Think of the situation that you're in, and ask yourself the question, *How fit is my spirit?* Because that's what's going to matter most.

When it comes to choosing your meaning of what's going on right now, it comes down to your spiritual fitness.

Let's remove the word *spiritual*. If you look at Maslow's hierarchy of human needs or Tony Robbins's six human needs... what's at the top of the pyramid? Spirituality. Self-Actualisation. Self-Realisation, and Self-Transcendence.

For so many years I've been practicing spiritual fitness.

I'm going to share something with you that if you never see me again, if you never hear my voice again, if you just keep doing this thing, I promise you it will keep serving you and you will keep *becoming* more than you are.

And that is the point of life: *becoming*.

Becoming everything that you can be.

Are you ready? Write *I'm ready* somewhere on this page.

I will go through the ingredients for spiritual fitness. I'm going to share it with you right now.

Here's what you've got to do.

Write this down: *Stretch goals.*

It sounds very simple, but having stretch goals has been one of the most powerful things in my life. As a coach, I have shared this tool with many people and it has changed their lives, relationships, businesses and, above all... their true *Why* for being here. Their true *purpose*. Stretch goals.

Let me explain stretch goals.

It's having a goal - a *physical goal* in this case, that stretches you to become a better version of yourself. When you take a piece of clothing and stretch it a little bit, it goes back to its original shape after being stretched. But if you stretch it enough with everything you've got, it tears or breaks... and can NEVER go back to what it was before! It can't go back to what it used to be.

A stretch goal is doing something you commit to that is so uncomfortable that it forces you to transform yourself just by committing to it and *signing the dotted line.*

It forces you to become someone new.

In my years as a coach, I have worked with many different people, including businessmen in their 30s and 40s that drink and smoke all week, and don't really believe that they can do more than what they're doing or have more than what they have.

Do you want to know what I do when I coach them? I sign them up to a stretch goal! A 10km run, a boxing match or an ironman triathlon. We find something that's personal for them.

I've taken coaching clients skydiving. And I've coached them right to the point where they're at the threshold between being in the plane… and out the plane, now free from their fear and limitations.

I've taken clients from average men and women to Ironmen and women doing running events, triathlons and even ultra marathons.

Actually, the cycle challenge that I did when I had my accident… I was doing with a client and now good friend, Callum O'Brien.

I have a question for you …

Have you ever *signed up* to a stretch goal - a marathon, cycle race, body transformation - anything that really *stretched you*… where the thought of just committing to that goal freaked you out, made you go sweaty under the arms because you were excited and nervous at the same time?

Did it change you as a person?

If it did, write *Yeah baby* somewhere own this page. If a stretch goal that you've had in your life *changed who you are as a person*… write *Yeah baby* now. Do it.

Fitness challenges are not about just the physical. They're about going on a *spiritual journey.*

What's Your Mountain?

Before we go any further, have you had any stretch goals?

Write them down. Take a moment right now. Write it anywhere. Don't read any further until you've written down something. Otherwise what I say next won't land.

By the way, the goal is not to set and achieve one stretch goal and think, *Yeah! I've changed my life forever.*

No, as you go to the next level, you will choose *another* stretch goal, then you'll get to *another* level and choose *another* stretch goal. The work never stops.

Let me give you an example of a stretch goal, and how you *become* in the process.

I am going to Tanzania and I'm climbing to the roof of Africa. I'm summiting Mount Kilimanjaro, the highest freestanding mountain in Africa, and I'm taking a small group of people with me.

The most important part of that journey, where some people might think it's the summit, is every single step.

It's every single step.

Some people don't want to climb Kilimanjaro because it's

a long way to get to the top. Yet, the fact that it is a long way, is exactly why you should do it.

Climbing a mountain is a movement meditation, just like running, walking, swimming and cycling long distances.

You are finding yourself in every single step. You are present with yourself. If it's a true stretch goal you won't be worrying about yesterday or tomorrow. You'll be 100% in the NOW. Which is the powerful place to be.

Who in the midst of a physical stretch goal thinks about their past relationship, or worries about next week's plans? No one. If you're doing those things, it's not a stretch goal, you're too comfortable.

You might tell yourself a fanciful story that's a stretch goal but it's not. If it was a stretch goal, it would require *all of you.* Every single part of your thinking, doing and being knows that this goal ahead of you is going to require all of you.

In the process, by digging deep and finding all you can be, you become more than you were, you become someone new. When you climb your own mountain, every single step counts because at the top of that mountain lies the centre of your heart. Your true highest self.

As you climb... grow... fail... learn... and keep yourself motivated and inspired to keep moving forward, you become a better, more conscious, more aware, self-transcendent version of yourself.

And you cannot stand on the top of that mountain and experience your highest truth unless you have climbed every step of that mountain.

(Note: I eventually climbed Kilimanjaro in October 2020!)

How Come?

People ask me, *JP how have you become a successful coach so quickly?* Personal Trainer... so quickly? Author... so quickly? Speaker... so quickly?

I've mastered a lot of things in my life, very quickly... and that's because I always attach stretch goals to my next big moves.

I have extraordinary belief in myself. Extraordinary mind, body and heart energy.

You can type *JP DeVilliers Accident* in Google and find the videos and press stories about my accident there. It's available for all to see.

You'll find my broken bones, the crash site… everything.

And you'll see that since my accident I've cycled 160 miles (250 kilometres), ran two half marathons and two marathons.

David Goggins is a super hardcore human being, and he's one of my role models. I love the guy. Great energy. David Goggins created a challenge called the *Four by four by 48 hour challenge.*

It's four miles every four hours for 48 hours.

For example, starting in the morning, every four hours run four miles - all day through the night, all the way through the next day, all the way through the night again. 12 rounds in under 48 hours. I took on the challenge and finished at five minutes to 4am.

Now, why am I sharing this with you?

Because it was like climbing the mountain. For me, it was a spiritual fitness journey. To the outsider, it might look like a physical experience, but to me, I knew it was going to be spiritual. Very spiritual.

And when I got to the 12th round, even though I'd documented the entire journey over those 48 hours, on that final round I put my phone away, because everything that I had done... every step that I took up the mountain in every round of running that I did with the very little sleep I had, was to get me to that place. *Everything that I had been through got me to where I was.* It was to be on that mountain and truly appreciate the view and to know my truth and experience all that I had become... not just in my run, but in my recovery from my accidents and in going though everything I'd been through in my life.

I let myself be 100% present in that moment. It was my moment. No one could ever experience it the same as me and no one could ever take it away from me. It was a truly beautiful and emotional moment.

This is the power of spiritual fitness.

You are able to live with extraordinary certainty, energy and obsession. But it's up to you.

Here's something I want you to act on.

I can't force you to do it. And I'm not here to sell anything or try to manipulate you in any way, I just want to help you. I really want to help you.

Let's say one more time… if you just start putting stretch goals in place in your life, they will continue to change your life over and over again.

Every new year of your life as you wake up on the first of January, do your very best to wake up *as you intend to live that year ahead*, because *everything is energy*, and how you start something is how you live something.

Meditate, exercise, get clear on your highest values, and then start setting your goals, where you are now and where you want to be. What do you want to do, and what stretch goal would catapult you forward in mind, body and heart?

Now, stretch goals is just one tool that I've shared with you so far. I've actually got 12 tools for self-mastery and spiritual fitness.

I'm coming to an end of this section soon. But I want to invite you to go deeper with me.

If this *feels* like the right thing for you to do, and you want to move forward… into self-mastery… and learn more about spiritual fitness, then I want to invite you to come with me, right now to the next section.

What's the value of this?

All I can say is this. When you have extraordinary energy, certainty, obsession … *you'll own your life*. Actually, the title of my last book is *How To Own Your Life*. When I was in hospital I had a few of my books with me to gift to the hospital team taking care of me and when I paged through my own book that I wrote a year before my accident… I thought, *Oh my God I wrote this for my future self.*

This will help you continue to keep growing and *becoming* in your life.

When you own your life… and you own your energy… in mind, body and heart… you don't have to sell yourself to anyone. Your energy speaks for you.

This is a promise I will make you. Because everything is energy. And people invest their energy in people.

Show up unapologetically, non-negotiably as you, with extraordinary certainty, energy and obsession for your passion and purpose.

If you want to live your life in this way, where you can do what you love and love what you do… and get paid for it… and you never have to force yourself on anyone, not even in a relationship… because you feel like you don't need anything… you want things, but you need nothing… then come join me in the next section.

There's a challenge in there.

Are you ready?

Part 2

Spiritual Fitness

"Spiritual Fitness is a term
used to capture a person's overall
spiritual health and reflects how spirituality
may help one cope with and enjoy life.
Spirituality may be used generally
to refer to that which gives greater
meaning and purpose in life."

Ref: https://www.navy.mil/docs/
SpiritualFitnessGuide.pdf

Thank You

Once again, I feel truly grateful that you're here and I'm humbled to be able to speak to you about changing your energy and changing your life.

I remember Tony Robbins saying if you read a book, or listen to an audio, or go to a seminar... and there's just one thing that you pick up that makes a profound impact... that you implement... then that is worth the time invested.

So, make sure you have a pen and paper handy. Make sure you're going to look for those golden nuggets of activity. Things that you can do. Things you will implement.

From here on in, look for those nuggets.

When I read a book I normally write my notes on the very page where I am getting the energy. I look for those one or two or three things that I'm going to implement off the back of it. That's when the change happens. That's when you get real value from the transaction of learning. You engage too. Make sure it's practical.

Once again, I feel truly grateful that you're here. I'm humbled to be able to speak to you about changing your energy and changing your life.

Set your intention. If you're reading this, you're here to grow.

I just want to say… I will talk honestly. No fluff. No BS. Honest truth. But I want to be clear. A lot of people come to my events or come to me for coaching and they expect me to work magic. I say, *If you expect me to spray magic dust on you or to wave my magic wand on your life you've come to the wrong event, so please leave now, because I'm here to make sure that YOU do the work. I won't do it for you.*

And then, on the first break, one or two people always leave the room, because they know they're not going to get the magic dust they came for.

I'm going to share how you can do great things. But the key is what I just said: do great things. The key is *the do*. If you are this far into the book, then you're already showing up and doing the work.

Let's get *doing*.

Yeah Baby!

So that I know you're with me, can you please write *Yeah, baby!*

If you are all in, write *Yeah baby!* Write that in the book, so I know that we're all in this together.

This is why I say *Yeah baby!*, not because I like being silly, even though I do, but because I'm doing it for a good reason.

I love to help people feel good.

And when you say those two words it changes something in your energy, even if you were feeling bad before.

Just say these words, *Yeah baby!* What does that do to your energy? Does it lower your energy, or does it raise your energy? Write up or down somewhere.

Saying those words. Yeah baby. As silly as it sounds, does it raise your energy up? Or does it take it down? Up or down?

And the reason why I'm asking you this is because the conversation that we're going to have is about *energy*.

The time that we're going to spend together… is all about energy.

There's a very important first lesson here. I'm going to share so much with you but already there's a very powerful lesson here.

Those two words can take your energy up, if you let them. It can change the way you feel, raise your spirit. That's the power of our language. That's the power of our words. And two words.

Two silly words can change the way you feel. And the way you say them of course. Put some energy into it:

Yeaahhhhh baby!

Just so you know, the reference is from the Mike Myers comedy movie, *Austin Powers: International Man of Mystery* (1997).

As a coach, I'm incredibly conscious of how people use their language and I'm always encouraging people to mind their language.

I Need To Vs. I Want To

Here's another example. If you say, *I need to change my life, I need to change my life* then on a scale from 1 to 10, how positive does that feel when you say *I need to change my life?*

Now, I want you to change one word. One word, *I need to change my life* to, *I want to change my life.*

Say it three times. *I want to change my life. I want to change my life. I want to change my life.* It *feels* different.

Give yourself a score on a scale from 1 to 10. A 10 would be, it feels amazing... a 1 would be check for a pulse.

Now I'm generalising and I will do a lot of generalising in our time together because obviously I don't know you and I can't see your face ... but for me, saying *I need to change my life* feels around 4 four out of 10.

It feels positive but the word *need* makes me feel like I'm lacking something. There's some scarcity. There's urgency. Maybe even some anxiety.

That when I say *I want to change my life*... I feel nothing but good and feel nothing but inspired. I feel responsible and ready for action. I feel optimistic. And that's the difference that one word can make.

Like I said before, we're going to have an in-depth conversation about energy, and I'm going to be giving you my energy. Therefore, I ask that you give me yours. Stay engaged.

Make sure that every time you open this book that you're bringing your energy to this conversation.

I don't need to deliver a certain thing in this book. I can share with you whatever I want in whatever way I want. And what I do really want to do is give you the very best of me.

I promise you, what will help you get the most out of this book is giving me the best of you. Is that cool?

I wish I could see your face. But I can't. Let's decide to have an extraordinary experience anyway.

Okay, let's get started.

Change Your Energy, Change Your Life

Everything I've talked about in this book so far can be summed up this way: *change your energy, change your life.* That will be the continuous theme of our time together.

I've shared my story and I've shared a bit about what I've learnt having faced a near-death accident.

I am known today as a coach, speaker, athlete and author. I'm a plant-based athlete. I'm very passionate about kindness and compassion and even though I'm from Cape Town, South Africa (South Africans mostly live on meat!), I decided to go plant-based at the age of 35. I've eaten nothing but plants since 2016. No animals. How? It's been difficult making the shift after 35 years of eating meat.

But like anything in life, to be successful at something, you have to have a bigger *why* than the *how*.

If the *how* is bigger than the *why*, you won't make it happen. That goes for the same in business, fitness and relationships.

I've been in the self-mastery game since the age of 23. I've been obsessed about personal development, self improvement and learning about how I can be a better human being and leader to others.

How can I be the best version of myself?

Before I was 23 years old, when I made the decision to change my life,

I was doing a lot of partying and living a very hedonistic life. But then I decided to become the best version of myself. And I did it just for myself. That's what I've always done.

I take something on myself, see if it works and then if it does, I share it with others. I've studied all over the world with some of the best teachers, and I continue to study and change the teachers I learn from, as I continue to grow.

One of my teachers today is Lisa Nichols. Someone who has been a mentor and great role model to me over the years is Andrew Priestley.

Over the years... I've studied, I've learned and I've grown. And when I find something that has worked for me - and only when I find that it has worked ... and I can prove it ... and I can see the evidence - only then do I go and share that with other people.

So before we continue I want to be very clear with you. I don't *need* to be. And everything that I'm going to share with you is something that is tried, true and tested in my own life, first.

I refuse to learn something in a textbook or hear someone say something on stage, and then go share it because they say so.

Everything that I'm going to share with you I have practiced in my own life. I've found it to be of benefit and value to me first. And therefore, I have made it my obligation to share it with you.

That's what I do and that's what I'm known for.

Here's a quick recap about me and where I'm from...

I'm from Cape Town, South Africa.

I didn't have the greatest upbringing, but I found fitness as a way for me to feel good. And I used that until I was 19 years old when I found another way to feel good, which was partying and just living too much in the moment. That took me to London and I became a DJ. By 23, I was a full time DJ and on New Year's Eve I ended up DJing in Riga, Latvia.

Growing up as a child that didn't really have much, and always feeling like I was lacking something, now at 23 years old I'd created a life for myself where I was full of everything. I was swimming in a sea of consumption.

I was consuming opportunities, popularly, significance and even acceptance. I was consuming drugs and alcohol ... and women.

And when in Riga... at the end of all of that consumption on New Years Eve, the next morning, I couldn't consume anything more because I was too intoxicated.

And I was alone.

In that moment I realised that, *Man I'm getting life wrong.* I was on my own on the first day of the year, a day of celebration ... and I was feeling like I was suffering more than I'd ever suffered in my life.

In that moment I had a powerful moment of awareness *that if I could figure out how to get life wrong, I could figure out how to get life right.*

I went back to the UK and that's where my journey started at 23. Just for me. It was selfish. I didn't want to get life wrong. I wanted to get it right. Why? Because ten years before I had witnessed the ultimate version of getting life wrong.

My father - who shares the same birth date with me - the 27th of July - just a week after my birthday - my father committed suicide. He took his life.

And I knew at 23 that if I don't start surrounding myself with the right people, if I don't start learning the right strategies, and if I don't start thinking in the right way, maybe I'll end up going in that same direction.

And lucky for me that pain of being able to remember my father's death drove me to go in a new direction.

What drives us in a new direction or what propels us forward is running *away from* something or *towards* something. Running *away from* pain and running *towards* *pleasure.*

The pain was immense for me. And I was suffering.

I wanted to get to a place in my life where I was thriving.

What Needs To Change?

There is a technique in life coaching where you make a list of the areas in your life that you know you want to focus your attention on. (Search *Wheel of Life*). Things you want to change a little bit or a lot. It could be health, money, relationships, addictions, fun, relaxation, creativity... make your own list right now.

You know the areas of your life that need work, right?

Generally, most people will list health, relationships, career, fun, hobbies, recreation, education, financial, spiritual and personal growth.

You might focus your list on sleep, diet, weight, nutrition, play, life purpose, finances, spiritual.

Busy professional people often have a short list that includes relationships, professional life, career, personal, spiritual life and health.

A life coach will then get you to rate each area on your list out of 10. A 10 is the highest rating. The ultimate. This is the very best I can be. No issues at all in this area. This aspect of my life is amazing.

And a 1 means this aspect of my life totally sucks. It means this aspect of my life needs a serious amount of focus and a lot of work. (If you write 1, check for a pulse!).

So, make a list of the areas in your life that need work; and then rate yourself from 1 to 10 in those areas of your life.

Do this exercise right now on your own. Right now. Make a list right now and give those aspects a rating from 1 to 10.

I mean this.

OK. You are either *suffering, striving* or *thriving* in your life.

If the rating that you put is 1 to 3, meaning you feel 3 out of 10 in your happiness... or you feel 2 out of 10 when it comes to your abundance mindset... or how you think about money... or your relationship to money...

... it means you're *suffering* in that area of life.

For example, your primary relationship. How would you rate your primary relationship? If it's between 1 and 3 out of 10, you got some changes to make... immediately.

When? Immediately.

If you rate yourself from 4 to 6 it means you're *surviving* in that area. Just OK. Getting by.

You know how people say *I'm fine?* It's usually a 4 to 6.

Rating 7 to 10 means you're *thriving*.

Yeah baby!

Now the purpose of life is to thrive in every area. To be happy and feel good in all areas. Not perfect, but happy.

In romance... in relationships... social... friendships... in your finances... in your personal growth... in the fun that you have... in the environment that you're in... in your fitness and of course... your stretch goals.

The ultimate goal is to thrive in your overall happiness. In your overall happiness.

By the way, when I ask you to write, it's not for me, it's for you. When I ask you to write something in this book, on this page, now, you are *speaking your truth into existence.*

You are making a public declaration.

So now I want you to write down your score for your *overall happiness* of your life.

Where would you score yourself right now?

- 1 to 3: suffering
- 4-6: surviving. I'm okay. I'm good.
- Or 7 to 10: thriving. Life's amazing. I'm thriving in that area.

Write that down. Right now.

And then go drink a glass of water.

Truth Time

I want you to think about energy. Notice how even when you're writing the number in this book somewhere, it creates an energetic response in your body. Maybe also in your mind and heart.

By writing it out, *you speak it into existence...* you make it real. And you become more aware. *Awareness* is the first step to changing anything and everything.

A great way to raise your awareness is to ask yourself questions. As a coach, this is something that I'm very good at. Asking very good questions.

If you're reading this book and something has resonated with you ... if you're thinking I like what he just said... write *Yeah baby!*

When you write it down, you're affirming that you're in the right place.

Understand, knowledge isn't power. *Implementation of knowledge is power.* Taking knowledge and putting into action is power. So don't wait till the end of this book to get into action.

Write when I tell you to write.

If you're all-in, write *Yeah baby!* right now.

I confirm what you wrote … it speaks to me.

Commit to this. Get your energy moving. Get in the game.

Your Stretch Goal

In Part I I shared one tool to change your energy.

It was called stretch goals. Every year, have a big goal to stretch you to become someone new, stretching you to a point that you can no longer be the person you were before.

This could be a fitness goal or a spiritual goal...

Or a spiritual fitness goal.

I've lived in Buddhist meditation centres in silence for 16 days with no fitness, two meals a day, and no communication with any human beings whatsoever, meditating for 12 hours a day. I say that to share with you that there are many different types of stretch goals. How many days of those 16 days did I want to run home? Every day. Sitting for hours each day with myself was so incredibly uncomfortable.

At the end of making it through the 16 days of sitting in silence, I could no longer be who I used to be. I was changed. I was a new, better version of me.

I shared previously that I've run four miles every four hours for 48 hours, with the last run being at 3am in the morning. I turned off everything in the final moments of that challenge. I just stayed present and soaked up the moment, because I knew after facing myself, my limitations, my fears and my limiting beliefs for the previous 11 rounds over 45 hours...

I knew that in that 12th round, in that final hour that I could no longer be who I used to be.

This is the incredible power of stretch goals. I'm not going to go into it further, but I want to remind you that this is an important spiritual fitness tool.

What Is Spiritual Fitness?

First of all, physical fitness means a physical *state of readiness*. You can look it up in the dictionary. The definition of fitness, or physical fitness, is your *physical state of readiness*.

How ready are you physically? That's what fitness is.

The fitter you are, the more ready you are.

I love the saying. *Don't get ready...* I'm not going to say the rest. I want you to write the second half of that saying.

The saying is: *Don't get ready...*

Don't get ready - stay ready.

In May 2019, I was cycling across the UK for charity. I'd been cycling for eight days covering over 800 miles when I was hit head on by a hit-and-run driver. Thrown over the car, bike smashed to pieces. Thrown down a hill. Stopped by a tree and left for dead on the side of the road.

After lying there for an hour and a half, I was airlifted to hospital by helicopter and spent two weeks in intensive care fighting for my life.

The doctors said, *You're lucky you're so fit.* That was my physical fitness. My physical state of readiness meant that when I was hit by the car - bam! - I was ready. I was as ready as I could be to *fight for my life*, and I needed it more than ever.

What I'm sharing with you doesn't make me extraordinary. I live extraordinarily because of my extraordinary self-mastery tools. There are 12 self-mastery tools that I want to share with you soon.

Are you ready?

I am not different to you. I live an extraordinary life and I do extraordinary things… because of the extraordinary tools… and the extraordinary people that I choose to keep in my life.

I'm going to share some tools with you. Whether you use those tools or not, is up to you. But I promise you... if you use these 12 tools... or a selection of them, you will continue to up-level your life again and again and again and again, and again. And that's what's amazing about having the right tools.

If you live in a house with the right tools, you can keep fixing any problem over and over again. Only if you know how to do it, how to use it, and you hold yourself responsible and accountable to pick up the toolbox. Because you can't have all the tools but not ever use them and expect your life to change.

It doesn't work like that.

That's why I am here, calling on you to take action on your life.

There Is No One Coming To Rescue You Or Do The Work For You

No one is coming to rescue you. There is no rescue plan being put in place for you right now while you're reading this book.

And it doesn't matter how many seminars you go to or how many books you read or how many incantations or affirmations you use, *you have to do the work.*

Whether you're a student in school, a monk or a business manager... it doesn't matter where you are in life... there is always work to do.

Buddha spent his life sitting under a tree, meditating.

If I had been able to walk up to Buddha and ask him, *Buddha, have you arrived?* I'm sure he would say, *I've only just begun. There is still work to do.*

The same goes for Prophet Mohammed and Jesus Christ. I'm sure they would have said, *No, of course I'm not there, I'm still learning. I'm still becoming.*

You never stop growing.

You only ever stop growing if you choose to stop growing, and then because everything in life is moving and reinventing itself and growing...

If you are not... you'll get left behind... to die.

So, my call to you is to continuously stay in action. *Stay in action!* Keep growing. You might age, but you don't have to get old. You might get poor-sighted. You don't have to get poor-minded.

You don't have to depreciate in your life, your life can keep getting better and better and better.

If you choose it.

And I'm going to give you the tools to be able to make better choices.

I call it the MBA for your best life. The 12 pillars of your best life MBA.

A self-mastery and spiritual fitness MBA for living your best life, and it's about maximising and protecting your energy in 12 areas of your life.

www.bestlifemba.com

Stay in action. Every end is a new beginning. Age is a state of mind. Absolutely, aging is inevitable, but getting old is a choice.

I will never get old.

Get Your Energy Right

Getting your energy right in three different parts of your life is going to give you a good, health long-term relationship with your spirit. It's going to give you good *mind-energy*, *body-energy* and *heart energy*. Now.

Gifting yourself good energy now and using these tools in your life now is going to amplify your life. The three areas of your energy are: your mind, your body and your heart.

I want you to write down *Mind, Body, Heart...* because that's what we're going to get into.

We're now going to get into how to change your energy and own your life.

To truly live your best life, on your terms and not care about what others think. To trust your intuition. To go after what you really want. You have a high level of self-mastery where you have good energy in your mind, body and heart, you feel good... and you are happy. This is my definition of happiness.

My definition of happiness is this: *being crazy happy about where you're heading in your life and at the same time, before any of that comes your way, being crazy happy about where you are right now - happy chasing your future and happy about the present moment you're in right now.*

Being so present and happy in the now that your thoughts about your goals and dreams in the future don't stress you out. You live your life thinking it's already on its way.

That's my definition of happiness. And a fulfilling happiness is everything. What's the point of having a successful business or being busy always being busy...

You've got the house and the cars... but you don't know how to enjoy it? What's the point?

We've seen the examples of this in life where people seem to have everything on the outside, but they're dying on the inside. An example of this would be Robin Williams. Everything on the outside.

He had his own TV show. An award-winning, top rating sitcom. That gave him an amazing springboard into an impressive movie career. He won awards for being funny. Won awards for not being funny. He won an Oscar, the ultimate award... even though his whole life he was known for being funny. He had a beautiful family. But all of this success on the outside didn't equate and didn't equal the fulfilment level on the inside.

Another example... my own father, Gerry was charming, good looking, popular and successful at a lot of things, but inside he never felt enough.

He tried to take his life seven times and on the eighth time he succeeded.

His outer world didn't match his inner world. It's what cost him his life.

Let me share this with you... it's something I realised a few years ago and has become incredibly important in my life.

Whenever I'm chasing something or have an opportunity presented to me, or I'm questioning what I'm doing in my life, I always remember that success is what you see on the outside... and fulfilment is what you feel on the inside.

Don't do what will make you successful. Do what will make you fulfilled. Success won't necessarily make you happy if you don't feel fulfilled.

And the key there is **feeling.**

The ultimate goal in life is to be happy. Happiness is a feeling. It's not a bank balance. It's not a material possession. It is a feeling.

You don't say, *I think I'm happy.* You say, *I feel happy.*

Or you say, *I am happy.* You make that emotion who you are. You feel it so strongly that you make it part of your identity.

I am this emotion. When we feel things strongly, we make it our identity.

I am happy. I am in love.

It's a feeling you have.

And the opposite is also true. If you don't feel good, and you feel that with intensity, over time, you'll make it your identity.

Both require energy. You may not understand this but it's a choice. You get to choose where you focus your energy.

The rapper Will.I.Am said, *Do I give my energy to the dream or the nightmare?*

Coming back to what I said before about *suffering, surviving* and *thriving*.

If you can make your emotion, when not feeling good... your identity, you will reach a level of suffering. You'll believe that what you feel is who you are. And it's not true!

The goal of this book is to give you the tools to master yourself and to live with a high level of emotional and spiritual fitness.

Physical fitness is your state of physical readiness. Spiritual fitness is your state of spiritual readiness.

How ready is your spirit?

That's it!

And when I say spirit, I mean *all of you*. Your mind, your body and your heart is within your spirit. Your passions and your healthy obsessions are *in* your spirit, waiting for you.

Your spirit is all of your being. It is the collective. It is everything that you are now and everything you've ever been. You can be physically fit, but you can be spiritually unready. You can be spiritually broke.

I'm sure you know someone who is physically fit, but spiritually they're not in a good place. Maybe they don't feel good. Maybe they're not mastering their relationships. Maybe they are neglecting their intimate relationships, and therefore always at the gym.

Maybe they're having troubles in their life that they're not facing. Maybe their spirit isn't fit enough to be able to lean into life and handle what is being thrown at them. Maybe they don't feel ready to change their life.

How ready is your spirit?

I'm going to give you tools to become spiritually fit, to master yourself and your life and to start leading yourself in a better direction. But it won't happen overnight.

Hey... it could be, but by saying that it won't be... I don't set you up for an expectation that things will change fast. Persistence... and patience. That's how you play the game. Persistence and patience.

Your life doesn't just change. But it will change if you keep changing. It will change if you keep doing the work.

Physical fitness got me through the accident and got me through intensive care. It saved my life. I had heart trauma, had my torso cut open and insides operated on, had a punctured and collapsed right lung. My physical fitness got me through that.

My spiritual fitness got me through my recovery.

I'm going to share with you the 12 tools that I have built up over the last two decades of my life that I've relied on. Tools that are designed to develop spiritual fitness. Tools that were especially powerful in my recovery.

I hope it doesn't take a trauma to motivate you to develop your spiritual fitness. Best done now, anyway.

I'm incredibly grateful that I've been learning what I've been learning in my life, because it saved my life.

Your life might need changing. Or saving, too.

Mind Body Heart

First of all, I said we're going to talk about owning your life in three areas: mind, body and heart. And amplifying and optimising your energy in these three areas.

You're going to raise your energy and spiritual fitness so that you don't have to get ready. You'll be ready for what life has to throw at you.

These tools I'm going to share with you will continue to help you in your life.

If this has been good so far write, *Yeah baby!*

But before we move forward now, take a moment and reflect on what has resonated with you so far. What can you already see yourself doing more of? Less of? Better? Differently? What are you telling yourself? How does it sound? And what feels right? Are you getting a handle on this?

Take a moment to reflect.

Part 3

The 12 Pillars

Get The Most From The 12 Pillars

These 12 pillars… or aspects of self-mastery and spiritual fitness… are what I teach. I call them the tools in my toolbox. Twelve months of the year these are the 12 things that I'm always talking about.

And I want to explain just how powerful these tools can be. There's no point in me giving you a tool and not explaining it first and why the tool is so important.

Okay, let's get to it. To be very clear, these tools that I'm going to share are tools for you to bring yourself up to a higher place of self-mastery and spiritual fitness - a spiritual state of readiness. Always ready, always present, always living in your heart and not in your head. Always in love, not in fear.

I want to give you a great little hack for deciding what to do if you want to maximise the impact of using these tools. It's like the ultimate high performance hack.

What do you need to:

* Stop doing

* Start doing

* Continue doing

For example, if you are overweight what do you need to stop doing? Start doing? Continue doing? It's not hard for you to figure out your own performance plan. Try it out.

You might add the distinction of... What do I need to:

- Do more of/less of

- Do even better

- Do differently

Please don't tell me that you need anything more than this to start taking action!

And I'd add... test and measure. Try it out. Pay attention to what works.

In fact, pay close attention to what's working and do more of that.

I think I am borrowing from NLP here - the best five principles for success in anything that involves personal matters has to be:

- Ecological. In other words, it has to fit in with your life. There is no point focusing on creating wealth... at the expense of other aspects of your life such as ignoring your family or your health.

- Ethical. I don't want you doing something that is unethical, illegal or immoral.

- Respectful. Respectful of yourself and others.

- Defined by you. How would you like it to be? Make it personal. What do you truly want? All through this book I'm asking you to make lists and decisions about your life designed by you. I'm giving you some powerful tools but ultimately it's your life... not mine. I can tell you what works but ultimately you need to take on some accountability and step up and decide what is right for you.

- Holistic. Again, the benefits are distributed throughout your life, not just in one aspect to the detriment of other areas of your life. Success in one area of life can't come at the expense or to the detriment of another. Self-care underpins this principle.

Do you need much more than this to start figuring out what's best for your life? You will not become the best version of yourself if you don't take action ... or you succeed in one area of your life unethically, for example.

Study this section. (The first tool pretty much gives you the motivation and accountability for your own success). Figure it out.

Look, there are people who will tell you what to do. Exactly. But in a sense you are abdicating responsibility for your success. But you'll become the best version of what they think!

And there are people who say there's a short cut. Sorry. There are no shortcuts. We can collapse your learning curve - without a doubt - but I'd be lying to you if I said this it's easy or doesn't require any effort or engaged thinking on your part. You want a radical body transformation?

Sorry, you need to do the work.

Anyone selling you an easy, low road approach to success really does not have you or your best interests at heart. In my opinion and experience.

Got it?

OK. Here we go.

Mind Mastery

#1. Responsibility

The first tool is **responsibility**. Holding yourself responsible for *everything*.

Now, I believe that a great way to teach is to attach a story to the tool you're teaching. So I'm going to do my very best to relate this to something tangible.

When I was hit by the driver, it was a hit and run. He was intoxicated and he left me on the side of the road. I don't remember the accident, but when I eventually *woke up* I knew that I had a choice. I knew that I had a choice to either blame the driver ... or to take responsibility for where I was.

Now, let's just remember spiritual fitness is about getting to a place where you feel good. You feel good in your relationships when you're spiritually fit. And when you're spiritually fit on your own, when no one's around, you still feel good. You have a strong inner world.

I knew that I had a choice to either blame the driver for what he did to me - and looking down at my legs and seeing all the metal work in my legs and staples everywhere and stitches, pipes, the oxygen mask - I could blame him, but how good would that make me feel?

What would that do for my spiritual fitness, if the first thing I did was blame this person for doing what he did to me? And knowing that wouldn't make me feel very good. So, with my own tool of personal responsibility I had to make this my fault.

Like Nelson Mandela said, *Having anger or resentment is like drinking poison ... and expecting it to kill your enemy.* It doesn't kill anyone but you. I knew that I had to hold myself responsible, because for me to heal, for me to be okay, for me to move forward in my life in the best way possible, the only way I could allow myself to do that was to keep my personal power... and not give it away.

Too many people in life blame others for where they are. And in that blaming, they give themselves permission to be powerless and stay where they are.

Think about that.

I'm not saying these people who harm you or do wrong to you shouldn't be held accountable. They're still responsible for what they did. Your business partner is still responsible for ripping you off, but they are not responsible for how you feel as a result of what they did. That feeling is up to you. Why? Because it's not on the outside. It's on the inside.

No one can make you feel anything.

You cannot say something or do something to me that will make me feel less than I am or make me feel bad. How I feel is my choice and it is also my responsibility.

Whenever I can... I do my very best to hold myself responsible.

And I never blame. I never ever blame. I'm not going to talk about forgiveness right now. But, yes absolutely, forgiving is incredibly important. When you forgive others, really what you're doing is you're forgiving yourself.

I want you to think of the last experience you've been through or the experience you're in right now.

Maybe you lost your job. Maybe you don't have the money that you want. You don't have the relationship that you want. What is missing? What has been a disruption in your life? Think about what it is and then say this... *I am responsible. There is no one to blame.*

When you say this, you take back your personal power and now that you've taken your power back and said *I'm responsible...* you can change it.

#2. The Power of Team

The next tool is the **power of team.**

I'm sure you've heard that you are the average of the five people you spend the most time with. Most people know that you become like the people you hang out with. Most people know that you will be the average of the people that you work with and socialise with. Most people know that.

And you know, more than likely, that there are people in your life that when it comes to energy, are adding to … or taking from your life. Plus or minus. Most usually taking from your life when they should be adding to your life and wellbeing.

Now, go back to the first tool.

If the people in your life aren't giving you energy, aren't making you feel good or allowing you to feel good because it's not their responsibility.

If people in your life aren't making you feel good or raising your energy what do you need to do about that? Do you settle for that? Or do you change your environment?

Who you spend your time with and who you invest in is actually how you're investing in yourself.

I have traveled all over the world to get to the best coaches and the best speakers. Lisa Nichols, my coach, has become a friend. I've spent time with her in the US, South Africa and in the UAE. Only four months after my accident, I knew that Lisa was going to be in Johannesburg, South Africa.

And I knew I had to get there.

Why? Because you are the people you spend the most time with. I knew that I could get on a flight and that I would be OK, even though I was still on crutches and still in a lot of pain and discomfort. I went to Johannesburg for three days, from the UK, on crutches, on morphine because of all the metal in my bones, and all the surgeries I had.

I got myself to Johannesburg because I wanted to be around her and feel her energy. I wanted to get positive energy from Lisa. And of course I wanted to feel the energy of the room that Lisa was speaking in. It had 2,000 people at that event. I went there for the energy.

One of my mentors, Andrew Priestley, once said… Write this down…

If you're doing it alone, you're doing it wrong.

I want you to imagine you're in an arena playing a sport. This is a metaphor for your life. You're playing this sport and you're running in the right direction… with certainty, with energy, with obsession. But everyone on your team is running in the other direction! Everyone on your team. They're running backwards or sideways not realising what they're doing and that you're in the most important game of your life. The game of life. How well will you do in this game if this is the case? How well would you do? How well would you perform as a team?

You need your team on your side. If you've ever watched

a movie about sports… Where the team's losing… They're not playing together… They're not quite synching… It's not flowing. At halftime, they take them into the changing rooms and they give them an extraordinary motivational or inspirational speech. They speak to their hearts. They get them all on board. And then they go out there and they absolutely smash it, and they win. That is the power of team.

Remember the movie *Invictus*? Great movie about the power of team and the power of heart mastery.

You want to make sure that your team at work and at home is supporting your mission.

Our life is a game. And you are in the arena of your life, all the time.

You are in the arena… with everyone who's in your life. Some of the people on your team are your family. You're born with your family, but you don't have to die with your family. If someone in your family doesn't support your mission… keep loving them… but start loving them from afar.

I want to challenge you to think about how people in your life make you feel. Remember this: Life is short.

If you're not living your life being happy, you're living your life for someone else. If you're not living in your own happiness you're living in someone else's happiness, or even worse… you're living in someone else's misery.

Think about that.

I've had to reevaluate and reassess certain team players in my life many times and be willing to *let them go.*

If you're not on the way *with* me, then you're *in the way.* You're in the way of everything I want to become, everything

I want to be and everything I want to create in this world. Come with me or get out of my way.

The people in your life are either giving you energy or taking it away. If you're not responsible for the people in your life, you're not going to change them.

Mind Mastery tool number one is **responsibility.**

Mind Mastery tool number two is **team.**

#3. Meaning

The third tool for self-mastery and spiritual fitness is **meaning.**

There is no meaning in life. Do you agree?

There is no meaning. There is no exact meaning of what life means. You can have three people from the same environment, with the same family and get them to write what their life is like. You will have three different views. Three different perspectives. And that's because we create our own meaning. For everything in our life.

Look at your phone.

Some people will say this is an incredible phone. And some people will say, that's an old phone. But it's the same thing. We just create a certain meaning based on our rules for life and what we believe. We create our own meanings based on how we see the world, how we see others and how we see ourselves.

In everything that you're going through right now, you have a choice.

You have a choice. Decide... Is this the greatest thing that has ever happened to you? Or is this the worst thing that's ever happened to you?

When you lose someone you love... you have a choice.

Are you going to focus on what is missing? What are you going to focus on? What can you be grateful for, when that person was in your life?

I lost my cousin to cancer. For me to feel good whenever

I think of her I need to choose the best meaning for what this means. And I always choose to focus on gratitude.

I'm not religious, but I believe in God. I believe there is a higher power and I'm spending my life figuring out who God really is. For the purpose of this book, I'm going to call this higher power God.

When I feel sad, I think *Thank you God for reminding me of how much this person meant to me.* My sadness is their legacy. My sadness is a result of how much they meant to me. I must honour this sadness.

This has been a game changer for some of the people I've worked with. You being sad when you've lost someone is a beautiful thing. It's the legacy that they left in your life. The sadder you are the greater the legacy. The more you cry, the more they left with you. When you lose someone in the future,

I hope that you honour your sadness, because the more you feel the sadness, the more you'll be reminded of how important that person was to you. And eventually, that sadness and gratitude will turn to strength and power.

When you feel sad, say Thank you God for reminding me that this person meant something special to me in my life.

When it came to my accident last year, I chose the meaning that... this was the greatest thing that has ever happened to me. Here's why.

I've been coaching for most of my adult life. I've been a professional athlete in multiple disciplines. I have fought in Thailand in a stadium, I've run ultra marathons. I've done lots of crazy stuff. And this gives me the right and permission to share with people what I've learnt from all the experiences I've had. I've learnt an extraordinary amount about body and mind mastery.

Would you agree that some people go through moments of trauma in their life and then define the rest of their life by that moment of trauma? I knew that this could easily be me. And I wasn't going to let that happen!

For anyone who was already suffering because of a physical trauma experience, and anyone that might suffer in the future... I knew that this new experience in my life would give me permission to teach something new.

It gave me a new vehicle for me to inspire people to get through their own trauma and then in the future the tolls to help someone else. I've loved helping people my whole life. It's my purpose. I hate seeing people suffer.

I'm going off on a little bit of a tangent here, but if you're lost in what your purpose is, I want to share something with you that might help you.

The thing that you most want to do in the world already exists. Nature knows. Nature always knows and we are a part of nature.

So, if you are stuck with what it is that's your true calling, your true purpose... I want you to answer this one question and keep asking this question over and over. And notice what comes up for you?

What has been the main pattern in my life?

The main pattern in my life has always been fitness and helping people. The thing you've always wanted to be, do, have... your truest calling... your highest self... already exists in you. You just have to get it out.

Look back at your life and notice the patterns. They are there, I promise you.

I noticed a pattern in my life of always wanting to help people.

At my lowest low as a child at 10 years old when I was living in Cape Town, South Africa; we were so poor that my mother was getting food from my aunt (her sister), and I was wearing my cousin's clothes. My younger brother was wearing my clothes and my youngest brother was wearing his clothes. I didn't have a bicycle. My mom had a broken down car. We were having whatever was in the cupboard for dinner, including Weetabix or fish fingers on white bread.

It got to a point where my mother was selling chocolates door-to-door. My Mom proudly said to me recently, with a big smile on her face, *You know, I used to put food on the table from selling those sweets.*

My mother is one of the strongest women I've ever known.

I remember walking home from school one day and I had a tin foil wrapped strawberry jam sandwich. I didn't eat it at school.

I was walking from school and I saw a homeless man. He was in his 80s.

I sat down next to him on the pavement. Ten years old. I just gave him my sandwich. And we never exchanged words. We sat together in silence as he ate the sandwich. It was one of the happiest moments of my childhood.

I enjoyed that moment of being able to contribute something to someone. Being able to help someone, it's just something that I'll never ever, ever forget.

Back to my accident... All I've ever wanted to do is help people get out of suffering and now, because of my accident, I can help people *even more* than I've ever done in my life. I can now help people in the area of physical trauma.

As long as I do the work... I will have a new story to tell... and new tools to teach.

That is the power of meaning. To the outside world what happened to me looks like suffering. But to me it has been a beautiful gift in my life... and at the same time been the greatest challenge in my life.

Of course, it's been painful. I've got metal rods, pins, plates and nails throughout my body. I've got metalwork holding my arm and legs together. I've got scars all over my body. I'm still healing. But it has been a beautiful and powerful experience because the meaning that I chose to give it.

Whether a divorce, bankruptcy, amputation or loss of a loved one... You can't guarantee anything in life. Nothing outside of you is in your control. You will add to your suffering if you think life is unfair and that it *should* go exactly the way you think it should.

The only thing that's in your control is everything that you experience on your inside, including the meaning that you give your life.

The greatest way to live is to live believing that life is beautiful and to be spiritually fit means that you always believe that life is happening for you.

By God's will or your own will. With your attitude that

you bring to the world. To be spiritually fit means that whatever you are going through, you believe that it is always happening *for me*. You believe that life always happens *for you*.

And if anything is missing in your life then you believe it's already on its way.

That is the power of meaning.

#4. Focus

The final Mind Mastery tool is **focus.** What you choose to focus on.

This one really is about goal setting. It's about having clear *intentions* and focused *attention*.

Gratitude is the ultimate attitude. Write that down. Gratitude is the ultimate attitude. Nothing in life that you accumulate will mean anything if you don't feel grateful for what you have, because if you can't feel grateful for what you have now, what makes you think that you're going to be grateful for what you have in the future? What you do today is what you become. What you do every day is what becomes a part of you. Focus on what you can be grateful for... always!

Focus is broken down into *intention* and *attention*.

Your *intention* is where you want to go in life. What is your intention for being here? What is your *why*? What are your highest values?

Your *attention* is what you are doing now. *What am I doing right now? Is it taking me to my intention? Is it taking me towards my purpose? Am I living in my purpose?*

Your intention is where you're going. Your attention is what you're doing, day by day to get there.

You change your life one day at a time.

When it comes to self-mastery... You can control a day a lot easier than you can a week, a month or a year. What do you need to do today? Where does your attention need to be to be spiritually fit? Am I living according to my highest values and what really makes me happy? Are my habits getting me closer to my goals?

Ask yourself these questions daily.

For example, if your main intention in life is to feel good... If you wake up and you don't feel good and you're about to go do the same thing that you always do...

Stop! What do you need to do to change your day? What do you need to stop doing? Start doing? Continue doing? What do you need to do more of? Do better? Do differently?

Go to the gym? Meditate for an hour?

All of these tools are about feeling good. Self-mastery... Spiritual fitness... Feeling good. You have an abundance of energy and your cup is always full. Whenever you give to others you give them from the overflow, not from you being half empty.

Intention and *attention*. Know where you're heading... and then put your attention on where you are right now and where it needs to be. Don't over complicate it. When you over complicate, you procrastinate. If you over complicate in your life, you procrastinate in your life. And when you do that... you compromise your life. Remember KISS?... *Keep It Simple Stupid.*

Don't make things bigger than they need to be.

Imagine driving 1,000 miles and you're driving at night. You can't see anything in the distance, but you keep focusing on what's far ahead of you and what you can't see. Are you going to enjoy your drive? No. You're not going to relax and feel restful. You'll be anxious and even stressed.

The most peaceful, joyous, present experience you'll have when you're driving on that journey - the journey of your life - is when you look at the road in front of you, just ahead of you. You focus on the headlights in front of you and what you can see whilst driving at night.

And you don't worry about the rest.

Your *intention* is your life GPS. You know where you're heading. You're not worried about it, you're just looking at the road and the headlights in front of you and making the most of that experience.

That allows you to be more present in your life. The more present you become and the more patient you become, the better life you'll live.

Write this down.

To be present is to be patient and to be patient is to be present.

Have clear intentions for your life and your future. And put your attention on today because today might be the last day that you live.

Body Mastery

#5. Stretch Goals

By way of summary, let's look at the four tools in Body Mastery. The first one we've already discussed: **stretch goals.** Stretch goals are a big part of Body Mastery.

A stretch goal is something I recommend you put in place every year. It's a physical goal that requires you to stretch yourself on every level.

If you take a piece of rubber and you pull it a little bit, it stretches but when you release it the rubber goes back to the original shape. If you stretch the same piece of rubber and keep stretching it, it will stretch or even break... making it impossible to return to what it once was.

When you have certain goals in your life that stretch you, they force you to become someone new. A stretch goal that stretches you enough ... forces you to become someone better. Once you stretched yourself to a certain point it's almost impossible to go back to who you were.

Fitness is my thing. I used to be a fitness coach doing radical body transformations and because I understood the power of physical stretch goals and the impact they have across your life, I used to make all of my clients commit to at least one stretch goal while they worked with me.

When people sign up to a 10k running race... or run a marathon... or seven marathons in seven days ... whatever is a stretch for them they become someone new in the process.

When you first sign the dotted line on the application for that event, enrol in that course, sign up for that class or join a gym... whatever ... the point is, you commit!

Something happens in your body, even before you start doing the work. You've made a declaration - even if it's just to yourself. You are saying that you're going to step up and become someone new.

A stretch goal isn't about the goal. It's about who you become in the pursuit of achieving that goal, or even the attempt of achieving that goal, because even in attempting a stretch goal or not achieving it, in that process and even in the failure of that attempt, you still learn something about yourself.

Stretch goals are about challenging yourself to see what you're capable of. About instilling new belief in you that you can make the impossible become possible. Improving your life over and over again.

If you choose to walk this path, I'm going to ask you to *choose one big stretch goal - a physical stretch goal -* and step up and commit. Go public. And then follow through.

The intention isn't just achieving the stretch goal. The intention is to become the best version of yourself.

Stretch goals are about becoming. Life is about becoming, whether it's becoming more influential, more successful, becoming loving or becoming your truthful self. Life is about becoming, That's the journey.

What and who am I *becoming* in my life?

Stretch goals accelerate that process of becoming.

It's not going to be comfortable. It's going to stretch you to the end of what you think is possible. And you will become someone new at the other end.

If you've never done any kind of endurance event... you already know how much of a stretch goal it is. Signing up to do an Ironman triathlon is a hell of a stretch on your body, mind and heart, but you become someone new at the other end.

If you want to go live in silence in a Shaolin Temple or Buddhist Monastery for a month, that's going to stretch you! It will challenge you and flush out your limiting beliefs. Your current mindset will scream No! It will scream *Run, run, run, run run away! Why did you agree to do this? This wasn't for you! This is stupid. This was a dumb idea! You shouldn't have signed up! You're going to look like an idiot! You will fail! You're too young, too old, too fat, too thin, not strong enough, too tall, too short, too black, too white, male, too female, too blonde.*

All of your inner BS will show up. All of that will come up for you. What a gift! Now you know what's lurking there in your subconscious.

Whenever your admonition starts with the word *You*, it's definitely your subconscious talking.

The problem isn't these thoughts. It's *believing* them.

But whether it's the Iron Man, or the monastery ... or climbing Mt. Kilimanjaro ... choose a big physical stretch goal and stay in that stretch goal.

You being able to stay in your stretch goal is you overcoming yourself again and again and again. Never give up, never give in. Winners never quit and quitters never win. If you want your life to change, you must change.

Here's the thing. I'm chatting with someone who's 16 stone - probably four stone overweight. And they say, *Well, that's all right for JP,. You're an athlete. You're a fitness expert. You eat "4 by 4 by 48" challenges for breakfast.*

Good point. Sometimes I speak to the ultimate desired outcome. But I'm not buying that. Sorry. Neither should you. Here's why not.

I have a massive cross section of people in my Best Life MBA coaching membership. A massive cross section of ages, genders, health and experiences. They all do stretch goals. They all do something that they know is a stretch for them.

Some do three month body transformation challenges, where they commit to the three months and post a *before* photo and then an *after* photos in the Best Life MBA online community. They make it public.

Back in the day when I was a fitness coach, that was the number one rule.

I wouldn't do a 12 week transformation without the photos because now you're committing to stretching yourself and becoming somebody that will do the challenge no matter what the result. It's about who you become.

In Best Life MBA, we do smaller stretch goals that run each month, monthly fitness challenges. It can be squatting, burpees or pushups. Your goal this month might be to do 100 squats in one day. You might attempt to do 100 burpees a day. Some of my students set a goal to go for a run every day for 30 days. Or 10,000 steps every day for a month no matter what.

This month, whilst writing this book, I've taught the group a 2,500 year old yoga practice called *The Five Tibetans* and the goal for everyone is to attempt to do these five exercises every day for 21 days.

Someone in the group is doing 25 pushups for 25 days instead. It's their goal, not mine. The first time they did three push ups and collapsed. But by day 25 they cruised through 25 push ups. You won't believe the difference that makes. You will feel different!

But for a big physical stretch goal... It's the 1st of January... Have you decided what your big physical stretch goal is for the year?

Your physical stretch goal might be an adventure. It might be climbing Kilimanjaro or to walk The Camino.

That stretch goal will naturally get you to start thinking ... imagining ... preparing for that.

You start to take on some responsibility. You start to focus on what might need to happen to make that stretch goal happen. A physical stretch goal should stretch you. It's not just about the goal. It's who you become by engaging in the goal. It's the why behind the how.

I often say, *It's not the thing that matters, it's the thing about the thing.*

When you're being stretched... You might learn about your limiting self talk. You might discover that your inner critic - which for most people is there whispering quietly do-nothings at you every day... starts yelling at you. You might find out who you are ten metres from your front door... on your very first shuffle around the block... because you decided to start training... for the London marathon.

Pay attention. Focus.

But enough! You need a physical stretch goal. A big one. Each year. If you understand, write *I get it.*

I just want to add one more thing.

A stretch goal for someone in their 40s or 50s and who says *Oh I can't do a plank because I have a sore back.* (No, you have a sore back … because you can't do a plank)… the stretch goal should be to lift yourself off the ground for four minutes, starting with only 10 seconds and give yourself 30 days. But if you say, *I can't,* this highlights your beliefs and reveals your identity. *I can't.* Or *I am not able to.*

When you get to the end of the month and you're able to say, *I can.*

This now changes you. It changes what you believe. I can do something.

I was teaching stretch goals even before I knew what stretch goals were.

When my fitness coaching clients signed up to do personal training with me, I would make them choose a stretch goal. Like running a half marathon, signing up to a boxing match or a 90 day body transformation. Something that they knew would be a challenge … for them. And then I would push them to go even higher. What they thought was impossible. Not even on the list. Not part of their identity. *What? Me? Half marathon? I'm not a runner.*

My best clients were actually my worst clients. Because once they chose and achieved their stretch goals, they realised what was possible and what they were capable of and realised that they didn't need me anymore because they knew to just keep challenging themselves to stretch.

They learned to keep pushing themselves and to keep becoming more and stretching more - on their own.

Stretching became a way of life.

#6. Habits

The next tool is **habits.** I've alluded to this already, but what we do every day ... is what we become. *What you do everyday ... is what you become.* You might want to think about *Responsibility.*

Most people know of the Ten Commandments, right? The Ten Commandments of the Old Testament in the Christian Bible (Exodus 20:2-17 and Deuteronomy 5:6-17, if you want to look them up.)

The Ten Commandments are not just ten rules, ten principles, ten rituals ... they are ten thou-shalt-not *commandments ... set in stone!* Set in stone. What does that mean? It meant they were non negotiable. Write that down on this page. *Non-negotiable. Non-negotiable.*

Write down *non-negotiable.*

We have bad habits but they are almost by accident. Random. Ad hoc. What are your positive, life affirming habits? Conscious, chosen habits?

What are the non negotiable habits in your life?

What are your ten rules for your life? Your ten principles? Ten rituals? Your ten commandments?

What are your ten non-negotiables?

Your habits are the ten things that you prioritise above all else, before you do anything else.

Your habits - your positive habits - are a choice. They are the things that you do religiously. You do them without thinking. They are automatic. Bad habits are automatic but there's no awareness there. I'm talking about ten positive habits. You have to get to a point in your life where you get to not have to think about them. They're like compound interest that grows and you benefit.

They're all the things that you're doing without thinking.

You're not consciously putting it there as an action. It's habitual. It's a habit.

Like, you have a pee in the morning, or a lion eats first thing in the morning, it's a habit. It's a routine. You don't have to think, *Oh, today I have to remember to go to the toilet. Oh, I must remember to brush my teeth tonight.* I really hope as adults who have grown up, you don't have to remind yourself to brush your teeth, it should just be by default.

I'm talking about consciously chosen habits.

Here's the key point.

If you have certain habits in your life that you don't believe are going to take you to the best version of yourself, you need to change them.

You change your life one day at a time.

I want you to do an exercise.

I want you to look at your daily life. Look at your life, day by day. I want you to write down what the ten activities, experiences, practices are that you do non-negotiably.

I'm going to give you some examples. I'll mix up good and bad habits.

I want you to write down your habits that you do daily - day-by-day, that are upfront in everything that you do.

Here are some examples... Remember, I'm mixing up good and bad. Don't get confused.

Thinking negative thoughts when you wake up. Daily fitness. Daily meditation. Complaining first thing in the morning. Having a coffee first thing in the morning before you drink any water... even though your body's been dehydrated for the last seven or eight hours. Not saying *I love you* to your family, every morning, meaning it, and dismissing them because you're too busy being busy. Leaving the house last minute. Getting to work two minutes after the time that you're meant to be there. Inspirational reading, praying, writing in your journal, morning stretching or exercise. Eating a nutritious breakfast. Skipping breakfast. Gratitude exercises. Dog walking. Learning something new. Watching the news.

Pick different times during the day. Skipping lunch. Eating takeaways. Watching TV. Watching porn. Drinking. Being on your mobile phone. Gossiping. Watching sitcoms for soaps. Or a steady diet of crime shows. Going to bed late. Stretching before bed. Evening walking.

Pay attention. What shows up every day that you know is good for you - makes you feel good. Or doesn't. You know this! You do know what is good for you and what isn't, right?

Let me share something in terms of energy. Energy is everything and everything is energy. And energy goes where energy flows. Energy is everything.

The reason why we need to sleep as humans is because we need to reboot our system and reboot our energy every night. We are evolving and while we're sleeping these little work men and women come out and go to work on ourselves every night and this requires water. The brain is a battery that runs on fresh water. Water is needed to regulate your internal systems. Fresh water. Not coffee. Not alcohol. Water.

So when you go to sleep, imagine the body's supply of water being emptied throughout the night and by morning... it's empty. Now you are in a dehydrated state. You are not energised.

If you now drink coffee, you're putting yourself in an even more dehydrated state. You now have even less energy so now you will be craving a fast energy source. Most breakfast cereals contain sugar. Maybe you put sugar in your coffee. You'll be going to Starbucks or a coffee shop and you're letting loads of sugar into your body. Ah, now I'm awake. No. Now you have loads of sugar in your body, because even with that coffee you're still not hydrating yourself.

Now let me ask you, and write down the answers. Remember it's a public declaration on your life. *What are the habits that you have, that you know are taking your energy away? What are the things that you do every day in your life that you know are taking your energy away?*

Here's a few I already mentioned. Complaining. Moaning. Feeling stressed.

Unless you are an exception to the rule, and there's always exceptions to every rule, checking your email while you're still in bed is not giving you energy. It's taking you out of the present moment and therefore it's taking your energy.

To not be present means to be in the future or in the past.

To be out of sorts, to be in a disrupted state, to be uncomfortable, to be unsettled means to not be present. When you are present, you have more energy, you have more space and more time. But an unsettled mind, of any kind, or an unsettled body means you're either in the past or the future.

So, what are the habits that you know are taking energy from you?

I haven't watched mainstream news on TV in over a decade. I'm very informed about what's going on in the world, but I don't watch the news.

I want you to write this down... Write the word *News* and put a plus (+) sign or a minus (-) sign next to the word news. An up arrow or a down arrow. Energetically... write it down...

Watching the news... does it give you energy or take your energy away?

You have a certain amount of energy every day. And you have a certain amount of time every day. And the energy that you have is being put into every single second of your day.

Why do we watch the news if it takes our energy away, the one thing that we need to be who we want to be?

You have 86,400 seconds per day. And like a bank account bringing that out to you, you're able to withdraw 86,400 seconds every day.

Your energy is spent and invested over that time.

Every time you're watching the news, you feel negative, you're having a fight, you're complaining, you're being stressed out… you are literally throwing your energy away. It's almost like you're saying…

Here, have some of my energy. I don't need it.

If you're having a fight and you're choosing to stay in the argument it's because you want to be right. You're just giving your energy away. When you fight you are in an energy exchange. You really want to ask yourself, *Do I want to be right?* and keep giving my energy away, or *Do I want to be happy?*

Sometimes to be happy, you must stop doing what you're doing and move in a new direction.

What are the ten commandments for your life? Your habits. Set in stone.

What are the non-negotiables for your life that will give you, day by day, the most energy? That will allow you to master yourself at the highest level, so that you can show up every day with Certainty, Energy and Obsession… turning you into the CEO of your life?

What do those daily habits need to be?

Take a moment now. Start now. Make a list. Think about it. What you do every day is what you become. Running one time … doesn't make you a runner. But if you run every day or most days, long enough, eventually you will make it your identity.

Going to church one time isn't enough to make you a believer. But if you go long enough you will call yourself a person of that faith.

Practice makes progress and progress takes us to a new area that we once weren't.

So look at your habits. Good and bad. What do you need to stop doing, start doing or continue doing? Make some better choices.

I want my clients to live their best life. Everything that I'm sharing with you I share in my online coaching community and I share with my one to one coaching clients. It's all the same stuff.

I get my clients to look closely at their life - their habits - and I get them to assess their life, day by day. And then we make better choices about how they would like their life to be.

They identify the habits that deplete them of energy. They decide the ten habits that will give them energy. They pick ten. Then they go do these ten things. Consistently.

You create the rules for your own happiness and fulfilment, your own inner success, your own physical and spiritual wellness and fitness.

If I'm your personal coach, then I'm going to hold you accountable to doing those ten things. You tell me the ten things that will give you energy and then don't do them... and I'm your coach, now you've got me in your face, asking *Please explain.*

You don't need me as your coach. Get someone to hold you accountable. Get into a community of like-minded, like-hearted people that have the same views and perspectives of the world on how we could be, and how we can be right now.

And then live by those rules and I promise you, even if you forgot everything else, and you just create, today, a set of ten commandments, ten non-negotiables, your life will start to change, day by day. And the better you get, the better you get.

OK, let's be clear. I'm talking about habits that give energy to your body. You cannot build a peak life or the best version of you if you are knocking on an empty tank. The mind is willing, but the flesh is weak type thing.

Habits live in this category related to Body Mastery.

Watching a steady diet of hours and hours of TV means you're sitting for hours. You're not moving. The energy is not flowing. Literally. And mentally it's exhausting.

Most crime shows are on between 9 and 11pm at night. If that show is violent or creates anxiety, that will deplete your energy. You are triggering adrenaline. Most people have adrenaline fatigue. A steady diet of *News At 10*, just before bed, is not a recipe for a good night's sleep. Checking emails or social media in bed is the worst bedtime activity most related to poor sleep. Rest. A good night's rest is linked to good energy levels.

So, go back over this chapter and make your list. And pay attention throughout the day.

#7. Fitness

The next tool is **fitness.**

It's pretty straightforward. I think you know by now, fitness gives you energy.

There's a tsunami of research on the benefits of exercising. Moving. Stretching. Resistance work. Jogging. Walking. 10,000 steps. Brisk walking. Swimming.

I've never heard anyone say, *I've just done a workout JP. I've just come from the gym and I just feel so depressed. My workout made me feel depressed.*

Or someone say, *I've just been for a run. It was depressing.*

Most of the time if not all of the time when you're in fitness you feel good, you feel more connected to yourself, you feel more connected to your heart, to nature and even to God... moving what God gave you.

Your body is the only vehicle that you have for life. You can't trade it in, you can't sell it for a new one. Your body is your gift from God. How you treat your body... is your gift to God.

Care for your body. Because how you do one thing is how you do everything.

Move every single day.

And I mean this. Every day. Even if it's going for a walk or doing ten minutes of yoga. *Everything in the world is energy and energy in the world is everything.*

Do you want to feel life is accruing benefits and plus signs? Or do you want to accrue negatives?

If you want to close a deal, you best have certainty. You best have energy. Because people can tell. People can read your energy.

When you see someone's face, you can tell what they've done that morning. You can tell when someone's exercised. You can tell when someone has exercise as a non-negotiable in their life. You can also see when someone clearly doesn't exercise or win their morning with fitness.

If we were in a seminar, I'd ask everyone to stand up right now. And I'd asked you to look around the room and tell me, *Who do you think has exercise as part of their life? And who doesn't?*

You would know.

You can tell by their posture, physique and their energy. Their vitality, their conviction in their eyes is different, because they put energy into their body every day.

So, every day. Why? Because if you want something badly enough, how often should you do it? Write this down. *How often should you do it?*

If you want something badly enough, how often should you do it? How many days a week, should you do something?

- If you want to be healthy and lean, how many days a week should you eat green vegetables?

- If you want to be free from discomfort and disease, how many days a week should you drink fresh water?

- If you want to feel more grateful, how many days a week should you practice gratitude?

- If you want to have a happy relationship, how many days a week should you tell your partner or your family that you love them?

Every day!

Another question…

If you know that exercise gives you energy… and certainty… and passion… and it's free… it doesn't cost anything… and it can take just a few minutes… then why don't you do it every day?

If you don't already exercise every day, then this is something for you to really think about.

If you know that doing a little bit of exercise every day has benefits … and you don't exercise … why aren't you doing it? Is it because you don't have the time? You don't have time to feel good? To increase your certainty and energy for the day ahead of you? …That makes no sense to me.

When I started out as fitness coach I had people asked me, *JP, what's the secret? How many days a week should I exercise? Is it three days a week? Is it four days a week?*

I never understood this question.

What do they mean - three days a week? Four days a week?

Do you just want to be good enough? Good enough should never be good enough.

If you're going to do something … do it properly. Take it seriously.

Be all in. Otherwise you're wasting your time and you're wasting my time. That's what I've been telling my clients for years.

If you want something good enough, you'll *do it every day.*

Do you want to have energy and vitality? Do you want to get ready and stay ready, be ready, so you never have to get ready again? Do you want to add more years to your life and more life to your years? If so, how many days a week, should you move your body?

Every day. Come on. Get real.

Your body is incredibly responsive. Start moving. Start gentle. If you've been inactive for a long time… going high intensity is probably not a good idea.

Get advice, of course. Consult your health practitioner (not necessarily your Doctor) about your readiness to include any fitness plan if you've been sedentary or inactive or if you have injuries.

I have injuries from my accident! But I was still able to design a fitness plan that incrementally took me from a walking frame… to crutches… to a short walk that left me exhausted… to a longer walk… to lifting a small tiny weight… to a little jog… to a quarter squat… to a stretch… to some modified resistance work… only every day. Every day. I keep moving forward. Rain. Hail. Shine. Hot. Cold.

So, come on. What's your excuse?

No time? BS! What's stopping you? TV? Social media? Sad. Irresponsible. Remember number #1, taking *Responsibility?*

Some people are addicted to their excuses. Does excuse-making drain you of energy? Totally. If you've got time to make excuses you've got time to go for a walk.

What more information do you need? What are you waiting for?

See #6 Habits. See #1 Responsibility. See #4 Focus. Any of the previous tools will help you.

#8. Nutrition

And that brings me to the final tool in body mastery, it's **nutrition.**

You are what you eat. You are what you eat every day, all day long, every week, every month, every year.

So, what are you eating?

Very simply put - what are you're eating? ... Is it giving you energy, or taking it away?

Now, I like a drink. I like tequila. Good Mexican tequila, with 100% agave. I like good champagne. But I am aware and responsible. I know how it makes me feel. It lowers my energy, so I don't drink a lot.

Even if I have a night out on the town or attend a wedding party or a celebration of some kind, what I do the next day is I do something to get my energy back. I go for a walk in nature, go for a run or do a workout, because I don't want that thing that I did yesterday to sabotage my today and tomorrow. When I fall off the wagon, I get back on... immediately!

You change your life one day at a time.

You had a shitty day? That's okay, you get another chance tomorrow. If you have a bad day tomorrow. That's okay, because you'll get to reset again 24 hours later, or 12 hours later. By having this mindset that you can change your life one day at a time, it makes it easy for you to change, but it also sets you free from your excuses and giving yourself a hard time.

I'm having a shit day today. That's ok.

Say this, today is just *one of those days.* Think back to #3 *Meaning.*

This changes the meaning of your day. You're no longer giving yourself a hard time and you're not creating the meaning of *I'm terrible, I'm pathetic, I'm off my goals again, I'm eating like shit.*

Don't make it bigger than it is! *It's just one of those days.*

When you say, today is just one of *those* days, what's the meaning that you've given it? Acceptance. Surrender. Surrender to the fact that today is one of *those* days.

So, the final tool in body mastery is nutrition.

You probably want me to give you loads of information in this nutrition section. No. Seriously. You know what foods to avoid. It's not rocket science!

Let's test this out right now. Make a list of ten things you know you should stop eating. Right now. You know, the foods that you know are in no way good for you to eat. Make a list. It will include processed food, fast food, takeaways, junk food, sugary foods, fatty foods, pizza, crisps, chips, biscuits, fruit buns, lots of bread, hamburgers, fries, soda drinks, hot dogs and donuts. High carb and high sugar foods. Come on, if you can't make your own list, if you are that unsure, where have you been living? How do you NOT know the foods to cut back on or avoid?

Basically, foods overloaded in carbs, fats and sugars. Foods with lots of additives.

I could go into a massive lecture on food science right here and talk about the composition of foods. But seriously, it's not hard. The body knows what it needs to thrive. You just need to listen.

So again, let's test this out. Give me a list of ten things you know you should include in your diet. No brainer, right?

OK, two distinctions.

First, most people need to drop their portion sizes. A slice of pizza isn't evil. Ten slices are ultimately going deplete you of energy because of the energy required to digest crappy food! Some foods you can eat a lot of such as salads.

If in doubt, eat in moderation... but eat sensibly.

I said I like a drink but I don't have drinking sessions. I know when I need to switch to water.

The second point is to drink more water. Increase your water consumption. Again, people obsess about how much. Everyone has an opinion. But figure it out for yourself. If you have four pints of beer ... drink for pints of water! If you have a cup of coffee ...have a glass of water.

Your organs are regulated by your brain. The brain is an electrical instrument. It's like a car battery: it needs fresh water. The only source of fresh water to the brain is your stomach. Water transfers through the blood barrier into the spinal column. If you drink coffee, the coffee goes to the kidneys and liver to be flushed and brings back grey water to the stomach. That's what is sent to the brain.

The brain then regulates the organs. Grey water makes the brain sluggish. Your brain needs fresh water. It runs more efficiently on fresh water. You partner with your brain to do a better job.

It's not hard to understand. Please don't get hung up on the science. Increase your intake of fresh water. Not soda water. Not colas. Not Juice. Water.

If you have allergies, go see a Nutritionist. Seek professional help. I don't know anyone allergic to fresh water.

Heart Mastery

Matters Of The Heart

Now lastly, I'm going into **heart mastery.**

Heart mastery is doing things in life that make you feel good. That open your heart.

Not in your body. Not in your mind. It's how good you feel in your heart.

I want to share with you four tools for you to feel good in your heart. For you to feel spiritual heart fitness.

When you live in your heart you're not focusing on yourself, you're focusing on others. You live for *Ubuntu*, an African saying, which means *I am because of you.* When you live in your heart you have the understanding that your life isn't actually about you.

If you think your life or your business all about you - then you're already failing. You will not get the most out of your life living this way.

Business is about love. Business is about innovation. About making the world better or making a world better … *or your world* better … or someone's world better. It's about taking what already exists in the world and improving it for the good of you, your family, your community or humanity.

Or taking something that doesn't exist in the world and creating it for the world to be a force of good and create something positive in the world.

Business is about love. It's about putting energy into the world that will benefit others. It's not about you. If you think it's about you, you will probably always be suffering. You might feel good as a result of having loads of money. You might have loads of success. But it won't last. That feeling won't last. You'll always want more.

When I say *It won't last*, I mean, the *feeling* of what it gives you won't last because eventually it will wear off. Eventually it will wear off and then what will be left? Nothing. All that you've accumulated for yourself is now not serving you anymore. What now?

Maybe *Consumption* was your plan, let me get as much as I can in my life. But it's the wrong plan. You need to change it to *Contribution*. Giving. Not getting.

If you live to serve everyone in your life, you will treat them as you would treat yourself. You would love them as you love yourself. You would care for them as you care for yourself. This will fill up your cup... and your heart.

I want to give you four ways in which you can keep spiritually fit and master this important aspect of your life, your heart.

#9. Share Your Truth

Share your truth. Share what you know. You don't have to know at all.

I promise you, I don't know it all. I have far from nailed life. I'm still learning. I'm still a student of life. There is still a lot I *don't* know. But I continue to share my truth and what I do know everywhere I go.

Sharing your truth, vulnerability, failures, mistakes, and wisdom that you've accumulated in your life that's unique to you, because only you can learn it in the way that you learn it. It will give other people permission to do the same.

Marianne Williamson said in her amazing poem in *Return to Love* that when you liberate yourself you give other people permission to do the same. And the whole world is looking to be inspired. The world is waiting to be liberated and led in the right direction. Will it be you who leads them? Whether personal leadership or organisational leadership. People are waiting to be led and inspired. And what inspires most… is truth.

So… speak your truth. The world is waiting for your voice.

Share your truth with others. Get on social media. Maybe

because of reading this book you've already started to know your next move. You've decided to commit to something, but you're thinking, *Oh, I'm not ready yet.*

Yes, you are ready, you don't have to know it all. Just move!

If you want to start helping others you have to start where you are... with what you have. That's enough. And then keep growing. Because if you start today helping others in whatever way you can, whether giving them a strawberry jam sandwich or doing a Facebook Live sharing your insights about something, it doesn't matter what it is, by starting today you're already one day further ahead than if you start tomorrow. You're already ahead!

Day one... you're already ahead.

So, take action.

#10. Live Your Life For A Cause

The next tool is to **live your life for a cause.**

What opens up my heart, makes me feel super grateful, spiritually fit and in love with life is raising money for charities. When you do something for a cause greater than yourself it gives you energy, inspires you and fills your heart. Choose something that resonates with you. Make it not about you, and watch what happens.

Even if your heart opens up just a little bit, it will open you up to a new way of seeing the world. It opens you up to new possibilities and allows you to get out of your own way because when you're doing something for someone else, you're not focused on yourself. You're focused on giving, not getting. And you push so much further. You do so much more. And it's so much more meaningful.

Have you ever noticed how negative people focusing on themselves all the time only become more negative? Have you noticed how people that talk about how poor they are never get rich? People that talk about how depressed they are over and over and over again... never get well.

Because whatever we focus on expands.

When we focus on contribution towards others, guess what we get back? Contribution! What we do for others is what we do for ourselves.

If you give love to others… What do you get back? More love. If you give energy to others… What do you get back? More love. In terms of energy, this can literally change your life. In a moment.

If you shift your focus from *getting*… to *giving*, then what will come back to you is more of that. If you want more in your life… give more!

When I started working as a fitness coach, I started studying energy. And I started to realise that energy is always in fair value exchange. Therefore, I learnt that… the more I give, the more I get.

And if I'm not getting enough it's because I'm not giving enough.

If you can't give money, give time. Give your energy. There's always a way to give. And the more you give, the more you get.

Going back to *Ubuntu*… When we do more for others we end up doing more for ourselves.

Live your life as an altruist. Altruism is about living your life for others.

I care for you as much as I care for me. I want for you as much as I want for me. I've already shared two ways for you to practice altruism. Share your truth with others and do something for a cause greater than yourself. Just do more for others and watch your energy and life change, forever.

#11. Teach

Tool number three in heart mastery is **teach.** Never, ever stop learning. And never stop teaching and airing what you know. Someone you haven't met yet is waiting for you to help them up.

Share what has worked for you in your life and share it with someone who could really use your help. There is always someone who can learn from you. Go find them.

One of my clients has a successful business, and I shared this with him about becoming more spiritually fit and living as an altruist so that he could feel happier and with his heart full. He wrote on social media that he'd like to mentor someone. And a young adult took up the offer. He now mentors this kid, just because he put out the request. What you put out is what you get back.

I asked him recently, how does it feel?

He said, *JP, it feels so good man, and it costs me nothing to be able to help this guy.*

There you go... another way for you to open up your heart, to have more self-mastery of your inner world and be more spiritually aligned to your highest self. Your truth.

#12. Make An Impact

The final tool is to **make an impact.**

You're reading this for a reason. As my amazing friend, teacher and coach, Lisa Nichols would say...

Standing at your own funeral, as you look at your gravestone ... between your birth date, and your death date ... is a dash. What do you want that dash to mean? What do you want that dash to stand for?

What comes to mind immediately?

As a result of reading this book, take what you can from this book and use is to make an impact. Make a difference. Make your life count. Wherever you can... Align your existence to something that would create a meaningful dash.

That's it.

Part 4

How Do You
Want It To Be?

Putting It All Together

You've got this far. Fantastic. This means you know my story and you know about the twelve tools for spiritual fitness and self-mastery.

Let's now put it all together.

One of the keys is the big physical stretch goal. You want to walk The Camino. You want to do a three-month body transformation. You want to lose four stone.

How do you pick a stretch goal and incorporate these 12 pillars into that challenge? What are the next steps once you have a goal and you feel you understand the 12 pillars? Remember tools exist to deliver an outcome: they are not the outcome.

What's the next step?

For me, having physical stretch goals is natural. It's obvious because I'm an athlete. I've been in fitness for most of my life and it is very natural to design stretch goals around physical fitness and physical energy.

People talk to me about their stretch goals. They say it will be a stretch to learn something new, acquire a news skill, learn to cook, play piano, learn how to read music, speak French or write a book. *Something they've always wanted to do.* Something they've imagined is really hard. These are all good stretch goals ... but the first one I'd love you to work on is a *physical* challenge because that changes everything.

If it's not a stretch and it doesn't challenge you every day, it's not big enough. It's not a real challenge.

When I was a fitness coach I was working with the body and the mind.

One day I realised just how important a physical stretch goal is ... because it's the platform for changing so many other things in your life.

It will change your energy - physically, emotionally, mentally and spiritually.

Most people want to achieve more in their life but don't have the energy to do so.

You don't change your life from the outside in, you change your life from the inside out. It's an inside-out transformation. That's what spiritual fitness is all about - *changing your energy and life from the inside out.*

The desired outcome of this book is spiritual fitness. I know that when you stretch you are testing your spirit. I want to push you to have a physical stretch goal. I'd like to invite you to come to Thailand with me and do a fitness bootcamp. Or climb Kilimanjaro. Or walk The Camino. Or sky dive.

I'd love for people to read this book and say *F**k it, I want to do an Ironman.*

I want to run the London Marathon. Or Boston Marathon. Or do a 4 x 4 x 48 Challenge with JP.

I'd love to take you on that journey. Where the talk and the walk line up.

I spent time with my students recently where I asked everyone to say why physical fitness - simply moving everyday - is so important. We came up with over 150 benefits of moving every day. A long list of great reasons.

Then I said to everyone, so why don't people do it? Two reasons. Lack of awareness; and lack of responsibility.

People don't hold themselves responsible. They play the blame game or the excuse game. They're not taking responsibility for where they are or where they want to be... and importantly, who they want to become. They say: *I should do this or I should do that. Not... I will. I choose. I decide. I am.*

You know the talk. *The spirit is willing ... but the flesh is weak.* Someone quite famous said that! [In other words, a rueful admission that you would like to undertake something but haven't the energy or strength to do it.]

That's the number one reason why I become so valuable to people I work with. I help them hold themselves responsible and accountable.

Dream a little bigger and come up with things that excite you.

Then commit.

Choose a goal that excites you. Be courageous enough to be excited. Or get excited ... again. Then have the courage to step up and use the tools, because the tools work.

I encourage you to step up and come on the journey. Dream big and come on the journey with me. And have the courage to use the tools yourself.

Look, there are lots of tools out there, agreed. And people are clever. They duck and weave around committing. I have cherry picked 12 tools that work.

I can explain the tools again and again but honestly, you have enough in this book to pick a stretch goal, commit and get to work… and to sustain you in making the attempt.

I got hit head-on by a car at 40 miles an hour. This is the tool kit I've been using in my recovery and to get back to a full life. My first big stretch goal was to get out of the hospital bed. To take a few steps on a walking frame. Then crutches. Little by little. Then walk unaided. Four steps exhausted me. Then it was just to sit down and stand up again. Then do a quarter squat … not even a squat. Bit by bit by bit, right? So what's your excuse? I'm climbing Mt. Kilimanjaro next.

If you want an experience of what it's like to embrace spiritual fitness… choose a physical stretch goal. Yes, have your other goals - learn French, learn to cook, learn piano - but start here with a physical stretch goal… And go for it!

Next, study the 12 pillars and cherry pick what tools will kick start the journey for you. I don't care what order you do them in. Or even if you use all 12. Just make a decision. Study the tools. One or several will resonate. They will grab you. You'll see the tool of choice. It will sound right. It will feel right.

Take responsibility. Re-read *Responsibility*. Reflect on why that tool fits your goal (it's obvious …) Maybe you need a team around you - a cheer squad … or fellow travellers.

Maybe you need to explore *meaning*.

Or *focus*.

Maybe you need to assess your *habits*.

Maybe you need a series of mini *stretch goals* to kick start your fitness ... or change your diet.

Or maybe you need to *share the truth* ... that a big goal scares you ... or better, excites you? Sometimes a breakthrough needs a break *with* ... the wrong environment ... habits ... a diet that slows you down.

Maybe you need to link your goal to a *cause*. A friend is walking The Camino and raising money for cancer.

Maybe you need to *teach*. Become a teacher and start leading someone in a better direction. Maybe you need to research your goal.

I wish I could give you the exact recipe. But part of spiritual fitness is *attempting*. Figuring it out as you go along. Finding what works for you and what doesn't.

Trusting that you can.

Part 5

Let The Handbrake Off

I Can't Because ...

People tell me they love the idea of spiritual fitness ...

But ...

They applaud me. They give me the theory and they nod and smile and say all the right stuff. They leave comments that *agree 100%* with what I am saying.

But...

The problem is not how adamant ... or committed ... or earnest you sound ...anything you say before the word but ... in your mind ... is now redundant.

You can't love the idea of spiritual fitness ... but then argue for delay.

Or take a rain check. Or have as nice-to-do-one-day goal. Or worse, make it contingent upon ... an *if/then* condition.

If I do X... *then* I will pick a big stretch goal ...

I have a big stretch goal...

But...

People tell me they have no time to dream. *Big or small.* But they have time to complain. And belly ache. Or bore people to death with their story of why they can't...

Their excuses.

They have time to read bad news... watch bad news... share bad news... immerse themselves in conspiracy theories... and whine about the economy ... and failure of their politicians ...

And they have time to recite the performance stats of their favourite sports heroes. Time to immerse themselves in the intimate lives of celebrities. And they have time to blob in front of the TV and gorge on a steady diet of crime shows every night. Or bang down six pints of lager.

Why?

As I said two reasons. Lack of awareness. And lack of responsibility.

People know they are wasting their lives blobbed out in front of the TV... *later.* But at the time? No awareness. They're ignoring their own awareness. Or dumbing down their awareness. *I'll do it later.*

When?

And people don't hold themselves responsible for their thoughts or feelings. Or decisions. Or choices. Awareness and responsibility.

They play the blame game or the excuse game. They're not taking responsibility for where they are or where they want to be... and importantly, who they want to become. They say: *I should do this* or *I should do that.*

But not *I will. I choose. I decide. I am.*

So, if it's true that you *can't*, then get a long list of all the reasons why you *can't*. As I said, my first big goal after my accident was to walk again. The tools that I used to achieve that are in this book. I lost my physical fitness.

I had to rebuild that.

Spiritual fitness gave me the fuel to try. Please don't tell me you can't when you can. It's an insult to everyone who has no choice.

Part 6

You're Supported

You're Doing It Wrong If ...

If you think you can succeed on your own, then you're thinking is wrong.

If you are doing it on your own, then you're doing it wrong.

You need someone that's inspiring you in this area of your life. In the area of becoming. You need support to raise your physical fitness and spiritual fitness.

You need a supportive community that is encouraging you to show up in that way. You need the right environment. Athletes thrive around athletes. Champions become champions around other champions. You need to look at where you want to go and who you need around me. And that's why I've created my global coaching community called Best Life MBA (BLMBA).

I'm always climbing the mountain to the centre of my own heart. Searching, falling, discovering, enjoying, falling again and I keep climbing and keep climbing, because I am looking to reach the peak of my own mountain and live my best life. Now and always.

And all of us are in some way or another climbing to our own peak on our own mountain, and at the top of that mountain lies the centre of your *heart*.

Everything that you can be in your life is there, in your heart. Not in your head.

Once you've discovered yourself, healed yourself and transcended your physical body, you become more than your physical self, you become your true spiritual self. You are a spiritual being having a physical experience, not the other way around. You're not a physical being having a spiritual experience. You are your spirit and your spirit is you.

I coach people in two ways.

While I only coach up to ten people a year one-to-one, my *intention* is still to serve as many people as possible.

I have an online coaching community called Best Life MBA. It's an online coaching membership where people are aligned with everything that I've just shared with you.

And I coach them through weekly Facebook group lives and Zoom coaching sessions. Also, we have a Whatsapp group that is full of energy. The community in this group push each other in fitness. They push each other in mindset. We do online fitness classes. Meditations. Breath work. I do live workouts. I have guest speakers and experts.

But we do it together, in different time zones across 15 different countries.

It's a high energy community. Not just physical energy but in mind energy, in body energy and heart energy. And I help people in this group to continue living their best lives.

Why do I call it the *Best Life MBA?*

Well, first of all, The M stands for Mind. The B stands for Body. The A stands for Altruism, getting to a place where you take your mind and your body and you use it as a vehicle to serve from your heart for the greater good.

I show up in BLMBA every week.

And I would love to invite you to join us. It's not like this in this book.

I am live and face-to-face. I get to see your face every week. I get to talk to you. You get to ask me questions. We can have a conversation wherever you are in the world.

If you can't make the weekly live sessions every session is recorded.

When you sign up you can find over 100 hours of recorded coaching by me, plus a lot of other extra coaching sessions other guests.

And every month we do a fitness challenge, getting you to use your body - the gift that God gave you - and to celebrate it. And to give you a stretch goal for that month, and every month. Something for you to work on. Sometimes it's skipping. Sometimes it's running. Sometimes it's burpees.

We are supporting each other. Pushing each other.

And you have a community of people from around the world that are all into the same stuff. Getting the most out of ourselves and out of life.

Now, it's not for everyone, but if you feel it might be for you then come jump right in and give it a try.

You can only be a part of the community if you show up. It is no use being signed up to a community and not showing up. It doesn't make sense. Right, so you need to be in that community.

I would love to invite you to join the BLMBA community so you can get the support you need.

Go to the website below for the details.

www.bestlifemba.com

As a coach, I know that to get the most out of people. I need to use a big stick... because when you're uncomfortable... that's when you change. That's where the magic happens.

That is my invitation. I've made my tools easily accessible for you.

I hope that you keep non negotiably and unapologetically climbing the mountain of your own life, to reach the highest level and best version of yourself. And I would love to climb that mountain with you.

Skip sitting in a therapist's office for the next five years. Stop setting goals that you're not going to achieve. Set the right goals and get your energy back.

Set the vision and create the legacy.

Don't be one of those people who start fast and then drop off because they don't have the ability to sustain their energy.

Energy is everything ... and not being spiritually fit, not mastering your spirit and your own energy... will look like this: a lack of momentum, a lack of consistency, a lack of discipline in your life, difficulty in decision making, never trusting your intuition, living your life for someone else because you don't have the courage, confidence and certainty to lead your own way.

Surely, if you've got to this stage of the book... you want better.

If you do not become the master of your own energy, your energy will become a slave to everyone and everything else - your job, your employees, your relationship that's isn't getting any better.

Other people will use and abuse your energy. If you don't take ownership of it, someone else is going to stake a claim on it.

If you don't set clear standards and lay clear boundaries even your best friends with their very best intentions will walk all over you because they don't know any better.

Raise your standards and put up new boundaries and state, This is what I stand for...

These are my non-negotiables...

Either get on the way *with me* or get out of the way.

Prime your mind, body and heart to become the magnet that attracts the right people, experiences and opportunities into your life.

When talking about leadership... Who's going to look up to you to be an inspirational leader if you're not inspiring? Is the way you live your life inspiring?

Don't be someone who has the Ferrari, the big house and the bank balance... but who is unfulfilled.

Don't be someone who says, *I wish I spent more time doing what I loved and had the energy to do more in my life.*

It's sad to say that a lot of people want to be happy, but when asked, *What would make you happy?* they don't know.

Don't be this person. Make the changes you want and need in your life.

It's through mentorship and guidance that people can make these changes.

You can ask yourself questions all day long, but if they're the wrong questions they'll take you to the wrong solutions.

If you're already on a journey with a coach, teacher or mentor, great. But if you want to go on that journey with me then I'm inviting you into my inner circle.

If it feels right, it probably is.

Now is a good time for you to go within and trust your intuition. You already know the answers. The answers lie within you.

Let me share a story with you…

I was living in Northern Ireland a few years ago and I saw that Lisa Nichols was speaking in Dublin at an event. I wanted to go to this event to hopefully meet Lisa. I purchased the most expensive ticket, because I believe you get what you pay for. You get from life what you put in. And I wanted to have the best experience I could at this event. The tickets were not cheap. But my intuition said, *You have to go JP.*

I got the ticket. I trusted my heart and made the decision. After I had already purchased the ticket… the company called me and said, *Can you get to Dublin the night before the event? With the ticket you chose you actually get to have dinner with the speakers.*

Guess who was sitting at my table? Lisa Nichols.

My journey with Lisa started that day. Since then I have

interviewed her, spend lots of 1:1 time with here, supported her events, travelled with her and even spoken on stage with Lisa.

Our life is being created in every moment, and in that moment when I decided to go to the event I had a choice.

Your life is a result of all the choices you've ever made. So, choose wisely.

Go with your heart and get out of your head.

I often talk about Lewis Hamilton going up to Ron Dennis (the former owner of the McLaren group) and tugging on his shirt and saying, *One day I'm going be world champion for you.*

Yes, it's fun following your intuition.

We're all here for one reason. We want to get the best out of ourselves, maybe we want to get the best out of our world. And that starts with changing our inner world.

I congratulate you for reading this book. I can only hope and trust that you will continue to show up for yourself. And that while you're here you will continue to take action and keep climbing your mountain. Sometimes action doesn't mean go faster or doing more. Sometimes action means doing less. Sometimes it actually means taking a holiday. Sometimes action means just taking the day off, or sitting a meditation, but it's all action.

It's all momentum. You're either in momentum, or you're standing still.

Keep moving.

One Final Message

Thank you for reading my book on Spiritual Fitness. I wish the very best for you in your life. If you want or need help on your journey, please do get in touch. I am here to help you.

Remember, awareness is only the first step to changing anything in your life. Awareness on its own is not enough… You must act on that awareness. It's only at the implementation stage that awareness becomes valuable.

So… get into action… and stay in momentum!

Do you want to work with me?

For information about events, speaking engagements and to enquire about working with me as your Coach, please email *jpdv@jeanpierredevilliers.com*

To your best life,

JP

Dedication & Thanks

I'd like to dedicate the book to all of the teachers in my life. My life today and who I have become is a result of everyone who has invested in me over the years.

I am forever grateful.

I want to thank Andrew Priestley for being an extraordinary influence in my life. Mentor, Role Model and Great Friend. Thanks, Andrew, for believing in me, always pushing me and having my back. This book wouldn't have happened without you!

And thanks to Kate McNeilly for contributing to the editing.

I would also like to show my appreciation for my wife, Jules who is always by my side supporting me in whatever way she can. I'm incredibly grateful to have had Jules with me during my recovery from the accident. Even the nurses at the hospital where I was in intensive care told me recently that Jules was extraordinary.

About Jean-Pierre De Villiers

High Performance Coach, Speaker, Author, Athlete

- JP coaches clients to perform at their very best. He delivers high-performance results giving you optimum energy, peak fitness and laser-like focus.

- With two decades of experience in high performance and personal coaching, JP is renowned for running transformational events, seminars and challenges globally, stretching people like you to be their absolute best.

- He has worked with CEOs, Celebrities, Olympic Athletes and thousands of other key influential men and women, who demand the best from themselves, because they work in high-demand environments where their best is expected.

- Olympic gold medalists, business leaders, entrepreneurs, actors and award-winning film directors and producers all seek out JP's expertise and rely on him to help them perform at the highest level.

- JP teaches leading-edge strategies to keep you ahead of the game (and sometimes in the game).

- As well as speaking internationally, JP regularly contributes to publications and features in the media.

- He is the author of several books, is a professional martial artist, has completed multiple ultra-marathons and other endurance events and was voted as health coach of the year.

- JP was selected as one of the most inspirational London identities, supported by the London Mayor's Office.

- He has had the honour of speaking in front of the UAE Royal Family.

- JP has spoken internationally for Success Resources and Najahi Events.

- He has shared the stage with some of the world's best speakers, including Lisa Nichols, Jay Abraham, Mary Buffet, Prince EA, Jay Shetty, Robert Kiyosaki and Dr. John Demartini.

- He has represented the No.1 Success Coach in the world, Tony Robbins, throughout Europe, the UAE, South Africa and the UK.

Contact JP De Villers

Best Life MBA
www.bestlifemba.com

Coaching and speaking enquiries

jpdv@jeanpierredevilliers.com

Printed in Great Britain
by Amazon